PASTA
REINVENTED

PASTA
REINVENTED

Caroline Bretherton

CONTENTS

A FRESH LOOK AT
PASTA

WHY CHOOSE ALTERNATIVE PASTA?

Using non-traditional alternatives in pasta and noodle dishes offers complex textures alongside sophisticated and comforting flavors, as well as nutritional benefits for low-carb and gluten-free diets without compromising on taste.

EXPLORE NEW FLAVORS & TEXTURES

Non-traditional ingredients add a new dimension of texture and flavor to pasta dishes, from crisp vegetable noodles to earthy legume pastas. Less-familiar Asian noodle varieties, such as clear, crunchy kelp noodles and slippery, snappy shirataki, also offer new and unusual textures. The recipes in this book showcase the qualities of alternative pasta that make them unique, highlighting their distinctive flavors and textures with sophisticated sauces and thoughtfully paired ingredients.

CONSUME FEWER CARBOHYDRATES

You may be trying to cut back on carbs but still crave the comfort of a big bowl of pasta. Many pasta alternatives deliver all the satisfaction of your favorite dishes, but with far fewer carbs. Transform fresh vegetables into pasta-like ribbons, or seek out noodles made from yams, rice, edamame, and mung beans, which are ideal for those who want to limit carb-heavy grains. These lighter alternatives are equally delicious and satisfying, so you can enjoy your comfort food without the carb-guilt.

GET MORE NUTRITIONAL VALUE

Compared to their wheat-based counterparts, many alternative pastas provide more protein, fiber, and nutrients per serving. Legume-based pastas, such as those made from lentils and beans, have about twice as much protein as traditional pasta and three times the fiber. Pastas made from alternative grains are often more nutritionally dense than wheat-based pasta, while noodles made from fresh, raw vegetables are loaded with essential vitamins and minerals.

GO GLUTEN FREE

As more and more people eliminate gluten from their diets, the health food market has responded with a growing number of gluten-free options, including packaged pastas as well as gluten-free flours that you can use to make your own pasta dough. The recipes in this book show you how to use these new offerings to their best advantage, with seven gluten-free pasta dough recipes and many delicious dishes that feature different varieties of dried, store-bought, gluten-free pasta.

THE PASTA POSSIBILITIES

The many types of alternative pastas and noodles are as colorful and varied as the ingredients from which they are made. Vegetables, beans, and unusual grains replicate traditional pasta shapes, but have their own unique flavors and textures.

ALTERNATIVE GRAIN & NUT PASTAS

There are a number of widely available grain flours—many without gluten—that can add a new dimension of flavor to your pastas. Some alternative grains, such as einkorn, buckwheat, and rye, make rustic, earthy pastas, while others, such as rice and quinoa, are lighter and more delicate. Grain flour may be blended with a nut flour, such as almond meal or chestnut meal, for added flavor and texture. Look for packaged pastas at your health food store; they are available in many traditional Italian pasta shapes, and may be made with a blend of alternative flours, such as corn and quinoa. Asian markets are a good source for noodles made with alternative grains, such as buckwheat and rice.

LEGUME PASTAS

Flour made from dried beans, peas, chickpeas, or lentils can serve as a flavorful and nutrient-rich base for homemade pasta doughs, bringing all the healthy and delicious qualities of pulses to your pasta dishes. You can also find many varieties of pulse pastas at health food stores; these dried, packaged products often contain only one ingredient—such as black bean flour—and taste like the legume from which they are made.

WATER-PACKED NOODLES

Two alternative noodle varieties come packed in a water-filled plastic pouch—kelp noodles (made only of kelp), and shirataki noodles (made of yam starch). Both are traditionally used in Japanese cooking and have a very mild flavor that makes them perfect for soaking up spicy sauces. Because they are gluten-free and nearly carb-free, these noodles have become more popular and widely available in recent years. They can usually be found in the refrigerated section of the grocery store, near the soy products such as tofu and tempeh.

VEGETABLE NOODLES

Fresh produce such as zucchini and yellow squash create healthful pasta replacements—these are tender and hold their shape well when cooked, and are mild in flavor, so sauces and other ingredients can shine. More flavorful vegetables such as beets, butternut squash, carrots, and sweet potato can also stand in for pasta, and bring stunning color to the finished dish. There are a number of preparation methods that can transform your vegetables into attractive ribbons, long spirals, or sheet-like slices.

ALTERNATIVE GRAIN PASTAS

Many of the pastas in this book are based on flours made from ancient or unusual grains. Most are gluten free, and all bring their own unique flavors, textures, and nutrients to the finished dish.

BUCKWHEAT

This gluten-free grain is ground into a dark, speckled flour that has a rich, assertive flavor. You can make homemade buckwheat flour dough, or find dried store-bought varieties. Whether you want to prepare it Asian- or Italian- style, buckwheat creates a dense and nutty pasta that's best suited to lighter sauces. At the Asian market, look for 100 percent buckwheat soba noodles for the most nutrition and flavor.

CORN

Whole corn kernels can be ground into a slightly sweet and wonderfully flavorful flour that makes a delicate homemade dough. Corn flour is used in packaged gluten-free pastas as well—often as part of a grain blend, such as quinoa and corn—and can be found in shapes such as orzo, elbows, and shells.

EINKORN

This ancient wheat variety is high in protein, fatty acids, and other essential nutrients. Although it does contain gluten, it is considered to be more easily digestible than modern wheat varieties for those with gluten sensitivity. Einkorn pastas are available in a variety of shapes, and the mildly sweet and slightly nutty flavor works perfectly with a range of dishes.

MILLET

Whole grain millet has a subtle flavor that creates a lovely, mild flour. The cream-colored, gluten-free grain is an easily digestible source of fiber, protein, amino acids, and other nutrients. Whether you are using dried millet pasta or making lasagne sheets from millet flour dough, its mild taste enhances the other ingredients in your dish. Look for options such as millet spaghetti or millet and rice spirals.

OAT

Subtle and sweet, gluten-free whole oats can be milled to make a hearty flour that is a good source of dietary fiber and protein, and also helps to reduce cholesterol levels for heart health. Look for oat noodles—which usually contain a blend of wheat flour and oat flour—at Asian markets.

QUINOA

This nutritious supergrain is a great source of folate, magnesium, iron, and protein. Quinoa (technically a seed) is an ingredient in many versatile gluten-free pastas or noodles. It pairs well with savory dishes and a range of aromatic and sweet herbs and spices. Quinoa is often blended with other grains or legumes, such as rice or lentils, to make gluten-free pasta in a variety of shapes.

RICE

This versatile grain is used to produce a wide range of dried pasta and noodle varieties, from gluten-free Italian shapes, such as penne and manicotti, to traditional Asian noodles, such as rice vermicelli and rice stick noodles. Rice flour is also a key component of many gluten-free pasta dough recipes, where its mild flavor and light texture help to balance more strongly flavored flours.

RYE

This member of the wheat family is a good source of fiber and protein. Its robust texture and flavor are similar to whole wheat, but with more pronounced sour notes. Rye pastas are particularly well suited to earthy dishes with lots of vegetables. Italian-style rye pasta is available online and in some health food stores, often as spirals or trumpets.

SORGHUM

Gluten-free sorghum has a light, mild, and sweet flavor. This grain is an excellent source of protein and iron. With its hearty, slightly chewy texture and subtle flavor, sorghum flour is a wonderful addition to gluten-free pastas. Use homemade sorghum flour dough for dishes with bold flavors.

SPELT

An ancient relative of durum wheat, spelt (which contains gluten) has not undergone hybridization, making it easier to digest than modern wheat. It is a good source of protein and fiber, and its slightly dense, chewy texture and nutty flavor are well suited to Italian-style dishes. You can find spelt pasta in many traditional shapes at health food markets, or you can use spelt flour to make your own dough.

LEGUME PASTAS

The flavor of pasta and noodles made with legume flours can range from subtle to bold, but they all contain lots of healthy protein and add interesting texture to your cooking.

BLACK BEAN

This gluten-free, dark-hued pasta is usually made with only black beans, and has a distinctive earthy taste that is well suited to dishes with Southwestern and Mexican flavor profiles. Like the beans from which it is made, black bean pasta is high in fiber, iron, and magnesium. Take care not to overcook store-bought black bean pasta, as it can become grainy or mushy.

CHICKPEA

Flour made from finely ground chickpeas (also called garbanzo beans) is high in protein, low in carbs, and gluten free. When blended with binders such as xanthan gum and tapioca starch, it can be used to make a versatile and mildly flavored pasta dough. Pasta made with chickpeas has a slightly nutty flavor and a texture similar to whole wheat pasta.

EDAMAME

Pasta made from edamame (soybeans) is loaded with plant-based protein and fiber. Most store-bought varieties of edamame pasta are vegan friendly and gluten free. This nourishing and delicious legume pasta has a mild flavor that pairs easily with any dish that calls for Italian-style spaghetti.

LENTIL

Red and green lentils are faintly peppery and yield a firm pasta that replicates traditional varieties. Lentil pastas are gluten free, and are high in protein to keep you full. Use lentil pasta for dishes with bold flavors. Store-bought varieties, sometimes blended with quinoa or rice, are often available in rotini or penne shapes.

MUNG BEAN

Mung beans are used to make cellophane noodles (also known as glass or bean thread noodles). The gluten-free noodles made from this legume are transparent and chewy, ideal for a variety of Asian cuisines. Although they are not particularly nutrient-dense, mung beans are generally suitable for restricted diets. Mung bean noodles are widely available in the Asian foods aisle of grocery stores.

NUT PASTAS

Milled almonds and chestnuts can be blended with other alternative flours to add richness and sophisticated flavor to your homemade pasta doughs.

ALMOND

Blanched almonds create a super-fine flour that is ideal for gluten-free and low-carb baking. When mixed with a binding agent, it makes a subtly sweet and lightly textured homemade pasta dough. Its flavor pairs well with a wide range of sauces, but is especially suited to those that are rich and meaty.

CHESTNUT

Made from dried chestnuts, gluten-free chestnut flour lends a light sweetness and earthy nuttiness to homemade pasta doughs. Because it does not contain gluten, it must be blended with other flours or binders to yield a dense and smooth-textured pasta that pairs well with spring vegetables.

WATER-PACKED NOODLES

These Asian noodle varieties are packaged with water in plastic pouches, and can be found in the refrigerated aisle. They are free of carbohydrates and very low in calories.

SHIRATAKI

Most shirataki noodles are made from just yam starch and water, although some brands may include tofu as well. They have a distinctive, chewy texture with a slight snap, and come in a variety of thicknesses. Virtually flavorless on their own, they take on the taste of the sauce in which they are cooked. Be sure to drain and rinse them thoroughly to remove the packaging liquid, which may have a slight fishy smell.

KELP

Made from seaweed, these clear, thin noodles have a mild flavor that lets the other ingredients stand out in a variety of Asian dishes. Kelp noodles are crunchy when purchased, but will soften with most cooking preparations, which often call for boiling the noodles. Drain the salty packaging liquid and rinse them well before using.

VEGETABLE NOODLES

Vegetable noodles are a healthy choice for both cold salads and hot pasta dishes. Any produce that's not too soft or juicy can serve as the base for a delicious and nutritious meal.

BEETS

Beets come in a variety of colors—red, gold, white, or even candy-striped—all with faintly sweet, earthy flavors to enhance your meals. Beets have wonderful antioxidant and anti-inflammatory properties, making them one of the healthiest veggie noodle options. Select medium-sized, smooth, and firm beets for the best cooking results. To avoid stains, it's best to wear gloves as you peel and prepare beet noodles.

BUTTERNUT SQUASH

This rich, orange-fleshed squash is packed with vitamins, especially vitamins A and C. When cooked, it delivers a sweet, mellow flavor and slightly soft texture to form a hearty pasta meal. Use only the neck of the squash to form spiral noodles or thick lasagne slices (and reserve the round bottom section for another use, if desired).

CARROTS

These roots make a sturdy spiralized noodle that tastes good both raw and cooked. Carrots are extremely rich in vitamin A, an antioxidant that protects your cells and helps maintain skin and eye health. For the best spirals, peel and trim off the narrow end. At the grocery store, look for carrots that are relatively straight, thick, and long. For a special presentation, seek out multi-colored varieties.

CUCUMBERS

Fresh cucumbers make beautiful spirals that are best served raw. Because of their high water content, the noodles should be patted dry as soon as they are cut. You may also choose to salt and drain the noodles, which will draw out moisture and add flavor. To prepare, cut off the ends, and keep the skin on to help the noodles maintain a firm shape.

SPAGHETTI SQUASH

As its name suggests, this pale yellow winter squash comes with the noodles already formed—once roasted, you can just scrape the flesh, and it will naturally separate into spaghetti-like strands. Spaghetti squash strands are firm, textured, and mildly flavored. It's a great low-carb pasta stand-in for Italian dishes.

SWEET POTATOES

Just one medium sweet potato delivers your daily requirement for vitamin A, plus plenty of fiber to keep you full. These delicious orange spuds are sweet and firm with a fluffy texture that's fantastic for both sweet and savory dishes. Sweet potatoes can serve as the base for gnocchi, they can be spiralized or sliced into thin sheets to replicate noodles, or you can purchase sweet potato vermicelli at Asian markets.

YELLOW SQUASH

This mild summer squash variety resembles yellow zucchini, but tapers more at the neck. Like zucchini, it is easily spiralized, creating a firm but yielding noodle that mimics the shape and texture of spaghetti. Yellow squash can wither quickly, so look for ones that have been recently picked. Small or medium squash have the best texture and thin, crisp skin.

ZUCCHINI

With its even, cylindrical shape and perfectly firm texture, zucchini is the most popular vegetable for creating noodles. Low-calorie and full of folate and potassium, they form a soft ribbon that holds shape well, whether raw or lightly cooked. Both the familiar green variety and the less-common yellow variety have a mild taste that suits almost any flavor profile. To prepare, slice off the ends, but do not peel.

CREATING VEGETABLE NOODLES

With a few kitchen tools, you can transform carrots, cucumbers, sweet potatoes, squash, and many other vegetables into noodle-like shapes, which can stand in for traditional pasta in dishes from spaghetti to lasagne.

CHOOSING YOUR VEGETABLES

When selecting your vegetables at the store, opt for the most uniform and cylindrical ones you can find. Root vegetables such as carrots or beets make hearty, firm noodles. They stand up well to heat, so you can use them cooked or raw in your "pasta" dishes. Vegetables with more moisture, such as cucumbers, require delicate handling so they do not become mushy or shapeless. These varieties are usually best served raw in noodle salads.

SPIRALIZER

This tool is a quick and easy way to turn vegetables into spaghetti-like "noodles." If you plan to work with vegetables with a watery core, such as cucumbers, find a spiralizer that removes the core as you work so that your dish is not too damp. Spiralizers vary in design and price, but many come with attachments that let you choose the size of your spiral, from narrow linguine noodle to wide fettuccine ribbon.

BOX GRATER

Use the largest size hole on a box grater to create vegetable noodles in seconds. Trim your vegetable into an even shape, then grate it all the way down the longest edge to make your noodle.

PEELER

There are several styles of peeler that can create different noodle-like shapes. A traditional potato peeler can cut wide ribbons of zucchini that mimic pasta shapes like pappardelle or lasagne noodles. A julienne-style peeler will replicate a julienne cut, creating very fine sticks that imitate spaghetti.

MANDOLINE

A mandoline slicer cuts veggies into very thin, even strips. This tool yields the most precise shape of all the methods. Depending on the blades available, you can make wide slices to use as lasagne noodles, or use a julienne blade to create narrow, long strands.

MAKE
YOUR OWN PASTA

HOMEMADE GLUTEN-FREE PASTA

Many of the pasta dough recipes in this book are gluten free, and may require some practice to get just right. With patience and a few special ingredients, you can create delicious, tender pasta.

THE PURPOSE OF GLUTEN

Gluten is a protein found in wheat flour that gives traditional pasta dough structure and elasticity, allowing it to be rolled, cut, and shaped with ease. Without gluten—or a gluten alternative—dough is fragile, brittle, and tough. A successful gluten-free dough combines naturally gluten-free flour, such as one made from rice, quinoa, or pulses, with one or more binding ingredients to mimic the role of gluten and give the dough a supple, pliable quality.

USING ALTERNATIVE FLOURS & STARCHES

In place of gluten, there are several starches and flours that serve as binders, and can be blended with the primary flour in order to help the dough come together. Tapioca starch, sweet rice flour, or potato starch can all serve as binding agents, but too much of them can make for an oddly textured pasta that's too sticky or gummy. Instead, use them in moderation along with your main alternative flour and add a teaspoon or two of xanthan gum or guar gum—both of which are powerful thickening agents, gluten free, and vegetarian. It is these that will replicate the actions of the gluten in the dough.

OTHER GLUTEN-FREE ADDITIVES

If you have an intolerance to additives such as xanthan and guar gum, try using ground flax seeds, ground chia seeds, or even psyllium husk powder, which are all natural alternatives to thickening gums. A tablespoon or two of olive oil will improve the texture of all pasta doughs, making them more pliable, and eggs will make them richer and stronger (the protein in the egg yolks helps for this), as well as enhance the color.

YOUR GLUTEN-FREE DOUGH

The alternative flours and binders used to make gluten-free dough can deliver wonderful textures and delicious flavors, but they will not be as sturdy as traditional pasta. Follow the recipes in this book, and add water at the end very slowly and gradually until you reach the perfect moisture level. When shaping your dough, have patience and treat it gently. If your gluten-free dough is particularly fragile, roll and cut it by hand to prevent breaking.

WORKING WITH FRESH PASTA DOUGH

Fresh pasta dough is simple and rewarding to make, whether you shape it by hand or with a machine. As you finesse your technique, you'll soon begin to recognize the look and feel of perfectly prepared dough.

MAKING DOUGH

Pasta dough can be made by hand, in a food processor, or in a stand mixer with a dough hook, depending on the type of flour used. In general, the easier the flour is to work with, the less kneading it will require to become malleable and ready to roll. More challenging flours, such as buckwheat, need to be well kneaded and will never result in a very soft dough. Most of the recipes in this book call for a stand mixer, which is easiest on the arms, but any of the doughs can be made by hand if you are willing to knead them well. Once you make the dough, the longer that you can chill it (1 to 2 days), the easier your dough will be to shape.

ROLLING & SHAPING

You can roll out pasta dough with a rolling pin on a well-floured surface, or with a pasta machine. A machine yields a smooth and even sheet of pasta, but it can be challenging to feed some of the more delicate gluten-free doughs through the machine. For these, roll by hand or use a wide setting on the machine, as the dough will begin to crack when rolled too thin. Whatever rolling method you use, the easiest shapes to make if you're new to home-made pasta are variations on ribbons: tagliatelle, fettuccine, or pappardelle. Other easy, hand-formed shapes include farfalle (bowties) and simple ravioli squares or rounds.

DRYING & STORING

Fresh pasta tastes best when cooked the day it is made, but you can also make it in advance and store it. A fresh ball of dough can be made up to 2 days before shaping; just wrap it tightly in plastic wrap and refrigerate. Fresh pasta that has been shaped can be tossed with a little flour, packaged in airtight plastic bags, and refrigerated for up to 2 days, or frozen for up to 4 weeks. To dry uncooked pasta that has been cut into ribbons, drape the strands over a pasta drying rack, keeping them separated for best air flow, and let hang until brittle and crisp. (If you don't have a pasta drying rack, use the back of a chair, clothes hangers, or a laundry drying rack.) To dry smaller shapes, spread them on a dish towel placed over a cooling rack, and turn occasionally until fully dry. Fully dried pasta can be stored at room temperature in an airtight container for several months.

COOKING

Whether fresh or dried, homemade pasta will cook much more quickly than packaged varieties. To cook, bring a pot of heavily salted water to a boil and add the pasta. Fresh pasta made the same day will cook in about 3 minutes. Dried or frozen homemade pasta will take longer to cook, about 4 to 7 minutes, depending on the shape. Cook your pasta until al dente, or still firm.

ADDING
FLAVOR & COLOR

You can experiment with a variety of additives to bring flavor, color, and texture to your dough, including seeds, herbs, spices, and even vegetable purées. Add these ingredients before the liquids and eggs, as they may change the amount of water required to finish the dough.

SEEDS

The main thing to remember when adding any seed is to use very small varieties, so that the doughs are easy to roll out. Chia seeds, flax seeds, poppy seeds, hemp seeds, and sesame seeds all work well as additions to dough. In addition, pasta that is cut can end up tearing along the sides if the seeds impede the line of the knife. Use the seeds sparingly at first, and try to work with complementary flavors but contrasting colors for best effect, such as adding dark, nutty flax seeds to a light-colored dough.

HERBS

Most herbs will lose their bright, vibrant color when cooked, but still add a slight hue and plenty of flavor. Finely chopped soft-leaved herbs such as basil or tarragon are easier to use than hard, woody herbs such as sage and rosemary. These tougher herbs are best cut extremely small before adding to the dough. Alternatively, you can cook them in oil to soften them and release their flavors, and then incorporate the oil-and-herb mixture into the dough.

SPICES

Spices such as ground turmeric, smoked paprika, or even matcha green tea powder can add a burst of flavor as well as a subtle color to your finished pasta dough. Whisk the ground spices into the flour before you start making the dough to ensure an even distribution.

VEGETABLES

Spinach is often used to create vibrant green pasta, and purées of other vegetables, such as roasted beets or carrots, can also be used for a stunning effect. Purées add moisture to the dough, but no protein, so they will not help it to bind together. To help the dough cohere, add the purée, then the eggs and oil, and finally only as much water as you need to bring it together. You can also purchase powdered vegetables from online retailers, which have the advantage of adding flavor and color without any extra moisture, enabling you to stick to the original measurements of eggs and water.

DOUGH
BEET & RICE FLOUR

The vivid red shade of this beautiful pasta works best with simple, translucent sauces that let the color come through. You can also use golden beets for an equally vibrant orange hue.

serves 4 // time 1 hr, plus
45 mins to chill // dairy free
// gluten free

INGREDIENTS

6oz (175g) beets

2 eggs

2 tbsp olive oil

½ tsp fine sea salt

8oz (225g) white rice flour, plus extra for dusting

4oz (115g) brown rice flour

2oz (60g) potato starch

2oz (60g) tapioca flour

1 tsp xanthan gum

METHOD

1 Cook beets with their skins on. Either boil them whole, or wrap them in foil and roast in the oven at 375°F (190°C). Beets are cooked when fork-tender, about 45 minutes. Let cool, then peel and roughly chop.

2 In a blender or food processor, process beets, eggs, olive oil, salt, and 1 tbsp cold water until smooth.

3 In the bowl of a stand mixer, hand whisk white rice flour, brown rice flour, potato starch, tapioca flour, and xanthan gum until well combined.

4 Create a well in the center of flour mixture. Pour beet mixture into the well. Attach the bowl to the stand mixer fitted with a paddle attachment and run on low speed until a dough forms, adding cold water a teaspoon at a time if too dry.

5 Change to a dough hook attachment. Turn the mixer on medium speed and continue to knead until dough becomes soft and glossy. This takes 3 to 4 minutes.

6 Turn dough onto a work surface lightly dusted with white rice flour. Knead by hand for 1 minute.

7 Wrap dough in plastic wrap and refrigerate for 45 minutes or overnight before rolling.

BEST FOR MAKING // hand-cut ribbons // farfalle // ravioli

DOUGH
SPINACH & MILLET FLOUR

*This fragile dough is great for adding a burst of green color to dishes.
It works well as lasagne and other less-worked shapes. Roll by hand rather
than machine for the best results.*

**serves 6 // time 15 mins,
plus 45 mins to chill
// dairy free // gluten free**

INGREDIENTS

2 tbsp olive oil

1 small garlic clove, crushed

2oz (60g) baby spinach

*6oz (175g) millet flour, plus
extra for dusting*

2oz (60g) sweet white rice flour

1 tsp xanthan gum

¼ tsp fine sea salt

1 egg, plus 1 egg yolk

METHOD

1 In a medium saucepan, heat 1 tbsp olive oil and add garlic. Add spinach and cook, uncovered, over high heat for 1 to 2 minutes, stirring constantly until spinach wilts. Set aside and let cool to room temperature. Don't drain.

2 In a large bowl, hand whisk millet flour, sweet white rice flour, xanthan gum, and salt.

3 In a blender or food processor, blend spinach mixture, egg and egg yolk, remaining 1 tbsp olive oil, and 3 tbsp cold water until smooth. Create a large well in the center of flour mixture. Pour spinach mixture into the well.

4 With a wooden spoon, gradually incorporate spinach mixture into flour mixture to bring dough together. Then work together with your hands to form a soft dough, adding water a teaspoon at a time if necessary.

5 Turn dough onto a work surface lightly dusted with millet flour. Knead for 2 to 3 minutes until smooth and elastic.

6 Wrap dough in plastic wrap and refrigerate for 45 minutes or overnight before rolling.

DOUGH
SORGHUM & SQUID INK

*This very rich pasta is best served in smaller quantities
as an appetizer or lunch dish. Squid ink is widely available online
and gives this dough a dark, striking color.*

**serves 4–6 // time 15 mins,
plus 45 mins to chill
// dairy free // gluten free**

INGREDIENTS

*2 x 4g (0.14oz) sachets squid
or cuttlefish ink*

4oz (115g) sorghum flour

3oz (85g) potato starch

*3oz (85g) white rice flour, plus
extra for dusting*

2 tsp xanthan gum

¼ tsp fine sea salt

2 eggs

2 tbsp olive oil

METHOD

1 Empty ink sachets carefully into a small bowl. Add 1 tbsp boiling water to ink and whisk well to amalgamate. Stir in 3 tbsp cold water and set aside.

2 In the bowl of a stand mixer, hand whisk sorghum flour, potato starch, white rice flour, xanthan gum, and salt until well combined.

3 Add eggs and olive oil to ink and whisk well to combine.

4 Create a well in the center of flour mixture. Pour egg and ink mixture into the well. Attach the bowl to the stand mixer fitted with a paddle attachment and run on low speed until a dough forms, adding cold water a teaspoon at a time if too dry.

5 Change to a dough hook attachment. Turn the mixer on medium speed and continue to knead until dough becomes soft and glossy. This takes 3 to 4 minutes.

6 Turn dough onto a work surface lightly dusted with white rice flour. Knead by hand for 1 minute.

7 Wrap dough in plastic wrap and refrigerate for 45 minutes or overnight before rolling.

BEST FOR MAKING // machine-rolled lasagne & ribbons // hand-cut ribbons // hand-rolled lasagne

DOUGH
CHICKPEA FLOUR

This nutty pasta is very pliable and good for fine shapes, such as angel hair. It has a subtle, muted flavor that pairs well with delicate and herby sauces.

serves 4–6 // time 15 mins, plus 45 mins to chill // dairy free // gluten free

INGREDIENTS

12oz (350g) chickpea flour, plus extra for dusting

2oz (60g) sweet rice flour

2oz (60g) tapioca flour

1 tsp xanthan gum

¾ tsp fine sea salt

4 eggs

2 tbsp olive oil

METHOD

1 In the bowl of a stand mixer, hand whisk chickpea flour, sweet rice flour, tapioca flour, xanthan gum, and salt until well combined.

2 In a small bowl, whisk together eggs, olive oil, and ¼ cup cold water.

3 Create a well in the center of flour mixture. Pour egg mixture into the well. Attach the bowl to the stand mixer fitted with a paddle attachment and run on low speed until a dough forms, adding cold water a teaspoon at a time if too dry.

4 Change to a dough hook attachment. Turn the mixer on medium speed and continue to knead until dough becomes soft and glossy. This takes 3 to 4 minutes.

5 Turn dough onto a work surface lightly dusted with chickpea flour. Knead by hand for 1 minute.

6 Wrap dough in plastic wrap and refrigerate for 45 minutes or overnight before rolling.

BEST FOR MAKING // machine-rolled lasagne & ribbons // orecchiette

DOUGH
BUCKWHEAT FLOUR

This pasta uses dark, nutty buckwheat flour to create a deep flavor. Mixing it with the more neutral tapioca and potato starches helps temper the earthiness of the buckwheat and bind the dough to create a slightly chewy result.

serves 4 // time 15 mins, plus 45 mins to chill // dairy free // gluten free

INGREDIENTS

10oz (300g) buckwheat flour, plus extra for dusting
3oz (85g) potato starch
3oz (85g) tapioca flour
1 tsp xanthan gum
½ tsp fine sea salt
2 eggs
1 tsp olive oil

METHOD

1 In the bowl of a stand mixer, hand whisk buckwheat flour, potato starch, tapioca flour, xanthan gum, and salt until well combined.

2 In a small bowl, whisk together eggs, olive oil, and ½ cup cold water.

3 Create a well in the center of flour mixture. Pour egg mixture into the well. Attach the bowl to the stand mixer and run on low speed until a dough forms, adding up to ½ cup cold water a tablespoon at a time if too dry.

4 Change to a dough hook attachment. Turn the mixer on medium speed and continue to knead until dough becomes soft and glossy. This takes 3 to 4 minutes.

5 Turn dough onto a work surface lightly dusted with buckwheat flour. Knead by hand for 1 minute.

6 Wrap dough in plastic wrap and refrigerate for 45 minutes or overnight before rolling.

BEST FOR MAKING // blecs // machine-rolled lasagne & ribbons // orecchiette // farfalle

DOUGH
CORN FLOUR

Lovely yellow corn flour gives this pasta the color of traditionally made egg pasta, but without any gluten. Corn flour dough is delicate, and best used for unfilled and less-worked shapes.

serves 4 // time 15 mins, plus 45 mins to chill // dairy free // gluten free

INGREDIENTS

12oz (350g) finely ground corn flour, plus extra for dusting

4oz (115g) white rice flour

2 tsp xanthan gum

½ tsp fine sea salt

2 eggs, plus 2 egg yolks

1 tsp olive oil

METHOD

1 In the bowl of a stand mixer, hand whisk corn flour, white rice flour, xanthan gum, and salt until well combined.

2 In a small bowl, whisk together eggs and egg yolks, olive oil, and ½ cup cold water.

3 Create a well in the center of flour mixture. Pour egg mixture into the well. Attach the bowl to the stand mixer fitted with a paddle attachment and run on low speed until a dough forms, adding up to ¼ cup cold water a tablespoon at a time if too dry.

4 Change to a dough hook attachment. Turn the mixer on medium speed and continue to knead until dough becomes soft and glossy. This takes 3 to 4 minutes.

5 Turn dough onto a work surface lightly dusted with corn flour. Knead by hand for 1 minute.

6 Wrap dough in plastic wrap and refrigerate for 45 minutes or overnight before rolling.

BEST FOR MAKING // hand-cut ribbons // hand-rolled lasagne // farfalle // orecchiette

DOUGH
ALMOND & TAPIOCA FLOUR

*This pasta is remarkably robust. The dough is easy to work with
and can be rolled out very thinly, by hand or with a machine. Its mild taste
lets other flavors shine, making it great for dishes such as ravioli.*

**serves 4–6 // time 15 mins,
plus 45 mins to chill
// dairy free // gluten free**

INGREDIENTS

*8oz (225g) almond flour, plus
    extra for dusting*
4oz (115g) tapioca flour
4oz (115g) potato starch
2 tsp xanthan gum
½ tsp fine sea salt
2 eggs, plus 2 egg yolks
2 tbsp olive oil

METHOD

1 In the bowl of a stand mixer, hand whisk almond flour, tapioca flour, potato starch, xanthan gum, and salt until well combined.

2 In a medium bowl, whisk together eggs and egg yolks, olive oil, and ½ cup cold water.

3 Create a well in the center of flour mixture. Pour egg mixture into the well. Attach the bowl to the stand mixer fitted with a paddle attachment and run on low speed until a dough forms, adding cold water a teaspoon at a time if too dry.

4 Change to a dough hook attachment. Turn the mixer on medium speed and continue to knead until dough becomes soft and glossy. This takes 3 to 4 minutes.

5 Turn dough onto a work surface lightly dusted with almond flour. Knead by hand for 1 minute.

6 Wrap dough in plastic wrap and refrigerate for 45 minutes or overnight before rolling.

BEST FOR MAKING // machine-rolled lasagne & ribbons // hand-cut ribbons // ravioli // hand-rolled lasagne

DOUGH
SPELT & CHESTNUT FLOUR

This moist dough rolls out beautifully, holds together well, and has a lovely, mild flavor.
Shaped into ribbons or lasagne, spelt and chestnut flour pasta is perfect for
classic Italian dishes.

**serves 4–6 // time 15 mins,
plus 45 mins to chill
// dairy free**

INGREDIENTS

*8oz (225g) spelt flour, plus
  extra for dusting*
4oz (115g) chestnut flour
4oz (115g) tapioca flour
1 tsp xanthan gum
½ tsp fine sea salt
2 eggs
2 tbsp olive oil

METHOD

1 In the bowl of a stand mixer, hand whisk spelt flour, chestnut flour, tapioca flour, xanthan gum, and salt until well combined.

2 In a medium bowl, whisk together eggs, olive oil, and ½ cup plus 2 tbsp cold water.

3 Create a well in the center of flour mixture. Pour egg mixture into the well. Attach the bowl to the stand mixer fitted with a paddle attachment and run on low speed until a dough forms, adding up to 2 tbsp cold water a tablespoon at a time if too dry.

4 Change to a dough hook attachment. Turn the mixer on medium speed and continue to knead until dough becomes soft and glossy. This takes 3 to 4 minutes.

5 Turn dough onto a work surface lightly dusted with spelt flour. Knead by hand for 1 minute.

6 Wrap dough in plastic wrap and refrigerate for 45 minutes or overnight before rolling.

BEST FOR MAKING // machine-rolled lasagne & ribbons // hand-cut ribbons // hand-rolled lasagne // orecchiette

SHAPING
MACHINE-ROLLED
LASAGNE & RIBBONS

Using a pasta machine can help you create perfectly smooth and uniform pasta shapes. This method works best with robust doughs that are less likely to tear.

INGREDIENTS

1 batch of pasta dough
flour for dusting

METHOD

1 Cut dough into 6 sections and work with one section at a time, keeping the rest covered with plastic wrap. Lightly dust your work surface and rolling pin with flour.

2 Roll out a section of dough into a rectangle that is no wider than two-thirds the width of the pasta machine and only slightly thicker than the widest setting.

3 Run dough through the widest setting of the machine 2 or 3 times until it looks smooth and glossy.

4 Continue feeding it through the rollers on progressively narrower settings until dough is the desired thickness, lightly dusting with flour between rolls if necessary.

5 For lasagne sheets, use a pastry roller or sharp knife to cut dough into the desired sheet size. Place finished sheets on a baking sheet lined with parchment paper, adding extra layers of parchment paper as necessary so sheets do not stick together. For long ribbons, change the attachment on the machine to the desired shape. Run dough once through the machine to cut the ribbons. Place finished ribbons on a baking sheet lined with parchment paper.

6 Continue to repeat steps 2 to 5 to shape remaining dough. Set aside in a cool place until needed.

TRY // almond & tapioca dough // buckwheat dough // chickpea dough // sorghum & squid ink dough

SHAPING
HAND-CUT RIBBONS

For more fragile doughs, roll and cut your pasta shapes by hand. This creates an artisanal look and prevents the dough from breaking. With this method, you have the ability to make your ribbons narrow like spaghetti or wide like pappardelle.

INGREDIENTS

1 batch of pasta dough
flour for dusting

METHOD

1 Cut dough into 6 sections and work with one section at a time, keeping the rest covered with plastic wrap. Lightly dust your work surface with flour.

2 Place a section of dough in the center of your work surface and dust both sides with flour. Roll out dough into a 6-in (15cm) square. Dust both sides again with flour.

3 Roll dough into a long rectangle about 1/16in (1.5mm) thick and 6in (15cm) wide, lifting frequently to release from the counter. Transfer dough onto a paper towel and set aside to air-dry for about 15 minutes.

4 Start with the long edge, and carefully fold the dried sheet at 2-in (5cm) intervals to create a flat, rectangular roll.

5 With a sharp knife, cut roll into narrow, folded noodles at the desired width. Approximate widths are as follows: spaghetti 1/16in (1.5mm); linguine 1/8in (3mm); fettuccine 1/6in (4mm); tagliatelle 1/4in (5mm); and pappardelle 3/4in (2cm).

6 Unfurl the pasta rolls and transfer to a floured baking sheet. Repeat the process to shape remaining dough. Set aside in a cool place until needed.

TRY // spinach & millet dough // beet & rice dough // corn flour dough // spelt & chestnut dough

SHAPING
HAND-ROLLED LASAGNE

These simple sheets give your lasagne dishes a delicate yet firm texture that is harder to achieve with a store-bought variety. Depending on how you prefer your lasagne, you can make these sheets as thick or thin as you wish.

INGREDIENTS

1 batch of pasta dough
flour for dusting

METHOD

1 Cut dough into 2 sections and work with one section at a time, keeping the rest covered with plastic wrap. Lightly dust your work surface and rolling pin with flour.

2 Roll out a section of dough, flipping and rotating it occasionally at first, until it is as thin as possible without splitting. Trim the edges to form a large, even rectangle.

3 Use a pastry wheel or sharp knife to cut the large rectangle into 6 x 3-in (15 x 7.5cm) rectangles.

4 Arrange the rectangles in a single layer on a baking sheet lined with parchment paper.

5 Repeat the process to shape remaining dough. If needed, cover finished sheets with more parchment paper and start another layer of sheets.

6 Wrap the baking sheet in plastic wrap and store in a cool place until needed. Lasagne sheets are best used the same day, but you can also refrigerate them overnight.

TRY // spinach & millet dough // spelt & chestnut dough // corn flour dough // almond & tapioca dough

SHAPING
RAVIOLI

*It's surprisingly easy to hand-make fresh and delicious filled dumplings.
Don't worry about making your sheets a specific size for these artisan ravioli—
you can even cut them into different shapes.*

INGREDIENTS

1 batch of pasta dough
flour for dusting
1 batch of filling (see p159)
1 egg, beaten

METHOD

1 Cut dough into 6 sections and work with one section at a time, keeping the rest covered with plastic wrap. Lightly dust your work surface with flour.

2 By hand or with a machine, roll out a section of dough into 2 sheets about 1/16 in (1.5mm) thick.

3 Place spoonfuls of filling in lines along one of the sheets. Leave enough space between fillings to allow for you to cut out shapes—usually about 1in (2.5cm) apart.

4 With a pastry brush, brush a little egg around the fillings.

5 Place the second sheet of dough evenly over the bottom sheet to cover fillings. Gently press with your fingers around each filling to seal it.

6 With a pastry wheel or sharp knife, cut out ravioli. Use a fork or a finger and thumb to further press down around the edges and firmly seal. Repeat the process to shape remaining dough. Set aside in the refrigerator until needed.

TRY // almond & tapioca dough

SHAPING
FARFALLE

From the Italian for "butterfly", farfalle is also called bowtie pasta.
These little shapes are easily formed by hand. You can use a crimped pastry
wheel to make them even more eye-catching.

INGREDIENTS

1 batch of pasta dough
flour for dusting

METHOD

1 Cut dough into 4 sections and work with one section at a time, keeping the rest covered with plastic wrap. Lightly dust your work surface and rolling pin with flour.

2 With the rolling pin, roll out a section of dough into a very thin, roughly rectangular sheet, about 1mm thick.

3 With a sharp knife or pastry wheel, cut sheet into little rectangles, about 1½ x 1in (4 x 2.5cm).

4 Along the long side, very firmly pinch each rectangle in the middle to form the bowtie shape. Place farfalle on a baking sheet liberally dusted with flour, and keep covered. Repeat the process to shape remaining dough. Set aside in a cool place until needed.

TRY // corn flour dough // beet & rice dough // buckwheat dough

SHAPING
ORECCHIETTE

From the Italian for "small ears", orecchiette are little bowl-shaped pastas.
In the method below, you use your thumbs to create the depression in each disc.
Orecchiette pair well with almost any sauce.

INGREDIENTS

1 batch of pasta dough
flour for dusting

METHOD

1 Cut dough into 8 sections and work with one section at a time, keeping the rest covered with plastic wrap. Lightly dust your work surface with flour.

2 With your hands, roll a section of dough into a ½-in (1cm) thick cylinder. Use a sharp knife to cut into ¼-in (5mm) discs.

3 Flour your thumb and press down into the center of each disc, twisting slightly as you press. Then balance the orecchiette on top of your thumb and use your other hand to gently press dough down farther around your thumb to form a small bowl shape.

4 Place finished orecchiette on a lightly floured baking sheet without letting them touch. Repeat the process to shape remaining dough, then cover the baking sheet with plastic wrap. Set aside in a cool place until needed.

TRY // chickpea dough // buckwheat dough // spelt & chestnut dough // corn flour dough

SHAPING
BLECS

*These large, flat, triangular-shaped pieces of pasta are often served simply with
butter and grated cheese to make a delicious, filling dish. Use a pasta machine to
roll the dough smooth and a crimped pastry wheel to create attractive edges.*

INGREDIENTS

1 batch of pasta dough
flour for dusting

METHOD

1 Cut dough into 6 sections and work
with one section at a time, keeping the
rest covered with plastic wrap. Lightly
dust your work surface and rolling pin
with flour.

2 Roll out a section of dough into
a rectangle that is no wider than
two-thirds the width of the pasta
machine and only slightly thicker
than the widest setting.

3 Run dough through the widest
setting of the machine 2 or 3 times
until it looks smooth and glossy.

4 Continue feeding it through the
rollers on progressively narrower
settings until dough is about 1/16 in
(1.5mm) thick.

5 With a pastry wheel or sharp knife,
cut dough into 3-in (7.5cm) wide
long strips.

6 Cut strips into long, thin triangles,
with short side about 1½ in (4cm)
long. Lay each blec in a single layer
on a baking sheet lined with lightly
floured parchment paper. Repeat the
process to shape remaining dough.

7 Cover the baking sheet with plastic
wrap and set aside in a cool place
until needed.

TRY // buckwheat dough // spelt & chestnut dough

SHAPING
GNOCCHI

*These soft dumplings, usually made with potatoes and flour, are very easy
to make—all you need is a sharp knife, a fork, and a cutting board. Gnocchi
are a light, delicate pasta that pair well with heavy and flavorful sauces.*

INGREDIENTS

*1 batch of gnocchi dough (see p164)
rice flour for dusting*

METHOD

1 To form gnocchi, place dough onto a work surface lightly dusted with rice flour. Cut dough into 4 sections and work with one section at a time, keeping the rest covered with plastic wrap.

2 With your hands, roll a section of dough into a long, thin cylinder, about 1in (2.5cm) wide. Cut cylinder into discs about ¾in (2cm) thick.

3 Roll each disc into a small ball in your hands, then place on the work surface and tap to slightly flatten. Place on a cutting board.

4 When all are shaped, run the tines of a fork over the tops of gnocchi to make indentations. Set aside in a cool place, covered with plastic wrap, until needed.

SHAPING
SPAETZLE

Pushing batter through a slotted spoon directly into a pot of boiling water forms a special type of irregularly shaped dumpling called spaetzle. This classic egg noodle is a chewy treat that goes well with richly flavored dishes.

INGREDIENTS

salt

*1 batch of spaetzle batter
  (see p68 or p178)*

olive oil, to toss

METHOD

1 Bring a 3-quart (3l) pot of salted water to a boil, and prepare a large bowl of iced water.

2 Holding a slotted spoon or colander with large holes over the pot, use another spoon to push batter through the holes into the boiling water. Cook spaetzle for 1 to 2 minutes until they float to the surface.

3 Remove them with a slotted spoon and put into the iced water. Continue in batches until all batter is cooked.

4 Thoroughly drain spaetzle. Toss with a little olive oil to prevent sticking. Set aside until needed.

PASTA SOUPS

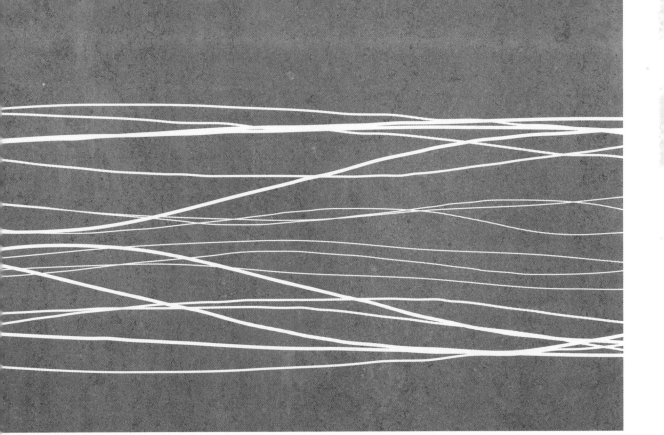

GREEN MINESTRONE WITH KALE & WALNUT PESTO

This bright, vibrant soup is made with a variety of fresh spring vegetables that give it a tender-crisp texture. Make sure to add them to the soup in the correct order, so they are all cooked al dente.

INGREDIENTS

4oz (115g) dried corn elbows or corn orzo

2 tbsp olive oil, plus extra to toss

1 small yellow onion, finely diced

1 celery stalk, de-ribbed and finely diced

⅓ large fennel bulb, finely diced

1 large garlic clove, minced

6 cups good quality vegetable stock

large handful of young green beans, finely sliced on the diagonal

10 asparagus spears, finely sliced on the diagonal

2oz (60g) frozen peas

½ small zucchini, halved lengthwise and finely sliced on the diagonal

for the pesto

2oz (60g) walnut halves

1oz (30g) young kale, washed, de-ribbed, and shredded

1 large garlic clove, crushed

2 tbsp lemon juice

12 basil leaves

4 tbsp olive oil

2 tbsp grated Parmesan cheese

salt and freshly ground black pepper

serves 4–6 // time 35 mins // gluten free

METHOD

1 To make the pesto: in a large, non-stick frying pan, dry-fry walnuts over medium-low heat for 3 to 4 minutes, stirring frequently, until they start to brown. Remove from heat. Once cool, rub them well in a clean dish towel to remove skins. Roughly chop.

2 In a food processor, pulse walnuts, kale, garlic, lemon juice, basil, olive oil, and 2 tbsp cold water to form a rough paste. Add Parmesan and pulse until you reach the desired consistency, adding a little extra olive oil if necessary. Pesto should not be completely smooth. Taste and season with salt and pepper, and pulse once more to combine.

3 Cook pasta according to the package instructions. Drain and rinse cooked pasta under cold water. Toss with a drizzle of olive oil to prevent sticking. Set aside.

4 In a large, heavy-bottomed saucepan, heat olive oil over medium heat. Add onion, celery, and fennel, and cook for 3 to 4 minutes, stirring occasionally, until soft but not brown. Then add garlic and cook for 1 minute more.

5 Add vegetable stock and bring to a boil. Add green beans and cook for 1 minute. Add asparagus and peas and cook for 2 minutes more. Finally, add zucchini and pasta and cook for a final minute. Taste and season with salt and pepper. Serve immediately, with pesto alongside for topping.

PASTA SWAP // dried quinoa elbows // dried brown rice ditalini

SEAFOOD NOODLE SOUP WITH DUMPLINGS

Kelp noodles become soft and delicious as they simmer in this soup, which is studded with savory herbed shrimp dumplings and bok choy.

INGREDIENTS

6 cups seafood stock

1 large lemongrass stalk, split in quarters lengthwise

1-in (3cm) piece fresh ginger root, thinly sliced

1 garlic clove, sliced

small handful of cilantro stems

2 tbsp fish sauce, plus extra to serve

juice of 1 lime, plus lime wedges to serve

10oz (300g) kelp noodles

1 large or 2 small bok choy, trimmed and cut into 1-in (2.5cm) wedges

for the dumplings

8oz (225g) raw shrimp, roughly chopped

½ tsp lime zest

2 scallions, finely chopped, plus extra to garnish

2 tbsp chopped cilantro leaves, plus extra whole leaves to garnish

2 tsp tapioca flour

salt and freshly ground black pepper

serves 4 // **time 50 mins** // **dairy free** // **gluten free**

METHOD

1 To make the dumplings: place shrimp, lime zest, scallions, and cilantro in a food processor. Process to a rough paste. Transfer to a bowl and stir in tapioca flour. Season well with salt and pepper. Set aside to chill in the refrigerator.

2 In a large, heavy-bottomed saucepan, combine seafood stock, lemongrass, ginger, garlic, and cilantro stems. Bring to a boil over medium-high heat, then turn off heat and let steep, covered, for 15 minutes. Strain broth, wipe out the pan, and return broth to the pan. Stir in fish sauce and lime juice, then taste and add more of either if desired.

3 Rinse kelp noodles under cold water, then let soak in cold water while you form the dumplings.

4 Roll dumpling mixture into 16 to 20 balls, and place on a plate. Drain and rinse kelp noodles once more.

5 Bring broth to a boil, then reduce to a simmer. Add shrimp dumplings and poach for 2 to 3 minutes, covered and turning occasionally, until firm to touch. Remove dumplings from the pan.

6 Add kelp noodles to broth and cook for 5 minutes over low heat, covered, until nearly soft. Add bok choy and cook for another 2 minutes until soft. Return dumplings to the pan and heat through.

7 Serve immediately, with cilantro and chopped scallions to garnish, and extra fish sauce and lime wedges on the side.

NOODLE SWAP // shirataki noodles // dried rice vermicelli // dried glass noodles

CHICKEN SOUP WITH HERBED SPAETZLE

This comforting soup is well worth the effort. Aromatic tarragon and fresh parsley create delicious spaetzle that sit in a rich and full-flavored base of chicken and tender vegetables.

INGREDIENTS

2 tbsp olive oil

1 small onion, finely diced

1 leek, washed, trimmed, and finely diced

2 carrots, peeled and finely diced

2 celery stalks, trimmed, de-ribbed, and finely diced

5½ cups good quality chicken stock

8oz (225g) finely shredded cooked chicken

for the spaetzle batter

4oz (115g) spelt flour

4oz (115g) all-purpose flour

½ tsp fine sea salt

½ tsp baking powder

2 eggs

½ cup plus 2 tbsp whole milk

1 tbsp finely chopped tarragon

1 tbsp finely chopped flat-leaf parsley, plus extra whole leaves to garnish

serves 4–6 // time 35 mins

METHOD

1 To make the spaetzle batter: in a large bowl, whisk together spelt flour, all-purpose flour, salt, and baking powder. Beat in eggs and ½ cup milk to form a very thick batter. Add remaining 2 tbsp milk if necessary, as well as tarragon and parsley. Beat vigorously with a wooden spoon until bubbles form. Cook spaetzle according to the instructions on page 60.

2 In a large, heavy-bottomed saucepan, heat olive oil over medium heat. Add onion, leek, carrots, and celery, and cook for 3 to 4 minutes, stirring occasionally, until soft but not brown.

3 Add chicken stock and bring to a boil. Then reduce heat to medium-low and cook for another 4 to 5 minutes. Add chicken and spaetzle. Return to a boil to heat through. Serve immediately, with parsley to garnish.

NOODLE SWAP // dried quinoa macaroni // dried corn orzo

MISO MILLET NOODLE SOUP WITH SWEET & SPICY TOFU

It's deceptively simple to make this seaweed-flavored stock. Add a pinch of bonito flakes for extra smokiness.

INGREDIENTS

10oz (300g) extra-firm tofu, pressed and cut into small cubes

10oz (300g) dried millet noodles

sesame oil, to toss and serve

2oz (60g) white miso paste

2 eggs, room temperature

3 tbsp sunflower oil

2 tbsp dried and crumbled wakame seaweed

2 tbsp roughly chopped cilantro

4 scallions, finely sliced on the diagonal

1 tbsp nori furikake

for the marinade

2 garlic cloves, crushed

1-in (2.5cm) piece fresh ginger root, finely grated

2 tbsp soy sauce

2 tsp sesame oil

2 tsp chili oil, plus extra to serve

1 tsp sugar

for the dashi

1oz (30g) dried kombu, snipped into small pieces

1oz (30g) dried shiitake mushrooms

serves 4 // time 1 hr, plus 1 hr for soaking // dairy free

METHOD

1 To make the marinade: in a medium bowl, whisk together all ingredients until sugar has dissolved. Add tofu, toss to coat, and refrigerate until needed.

2 To make the dashi: place dried kombu and dried shiitake mushrooms in a saucepan and cover with 8 cups cold water. Let soak for 1 to 3 hours. After soaking, bring nearly to a boil, but remove from heat just before it boils. Remove and discard kombu, and let dashi cool. Once cool, strain through a sieve lined with paper towel and discard mushrooms. Set aside.

3 Cook noodles according to the package instructions until just al dente. Drain, rinse under cold water, and drain again. Toss with a drizzle of sesame oil to prevent sticking, and set aside to cool.

4 Place dashi over medium-high heat, whisk in miso paste, and bring to a boil. Reduce heat to low and cover to keep warm until needed.

5 Place eggs in a small saucepan, cover with cold water, and bring to a boil. Then reduce to a simmer and cook, uncovered, for 4 minutes.

6 Meanwhile, in a medium, non-stick frying pan, heat sunflower oil over medium heat. Add tofu, scraping off excess marinade. Cook, without moving, for 2 minutes. Turn tofu over and cook for another 2 minutes until crisp and brown. Transfer to a plate lined with paper towel.

7 Increase heat under the dashi and bring to a boil. Portion cooked noodles evenly among 4 serving bowls. Peel and halve eggs. Pour the boiling dashi over noodles, and add wakame, tofu, and half an egg to each bowl. Sprinkle with cilantro, scallions, and furikake. Serve with sesame oil and chili oil.

NOODLE SWAP // spinach & millet flour noodles (see p30) // dried buckwheat soba noodles

BURMESE CURRIED CHICKEN & COCONUT SOUP

Curry leaves are a vital component in this version of khow, a traditional Burmese soup. They can be found fresh or frozen in most Asian supermarkets.

INGREDIENTS

9oz (250g) dried oat flour noodles
sunflower oil, to toss
2 tbsp coconut oil
1 small white onion, finely chopped
1-in (2.5cm) piece fresh ginger root, finely grated
2 garlic cloves, finely chopped
12oz (350g) chicken breast, cubed
1 tsp red pepper flakes
1 tsp turmeric powder
1 tsp chickpea flour
13.5fl oz (400ml) can coconut milk
2 cups good quality chicken stock
salt
handful of fresh or frozen curry leaves

for the toppings

1 cup sunflower oil
¼ white onion, finely sliced
2 garlic cloves, finely sliced
2 hard-boiled eggs, halved
1 tbsp finely chopped cilantro
1 lime, quartered

serves 4 // time 1 hr // dairy free // gluten free

METHOD

1 Cook noodles according to the package instructions until just al dente. Drain, then rinse under cold water and drain again. Toss with a drizzle of sunflower oil to prevent sticking, and set aside to cool.

2 In a large, heavy-bottomed saucepan, heat coconut oil over medium heat. Add onion and cook for 3 minutes until soft but not brown. Add ginger and garlic and cook for 1 minute more. Add chicken and cook for another 2 minutes, stirring often, until opaque all over.

3 Add red pepper flakes and turmeric and cook for 1 minute until fragrant. Stir in chickpea flour, then gradually blend in coconut milk. Add chicken stock and bring to a boil. Taste and season with salt. Add curry leaves and reduce heat to a simmer. Cook, covered, for 5 minutes, then turn off heat and leave to steep.

4 When soup is cooked, to deep-fry the toppings: in a small saucepan, heat sunflower oil over medium-high heat. It is ready when a small piece of noodle dropped in sizzles immediately. Take a handful of cooked and cooled noodles and dry them well. Place carefully in oil and deep-fry until crisp. Remove with a slotted spoon and transfer to a plate lined with paper towel to drain.

5 Using the same method, deep-fry onion, and then separately deep-fry garlic. The garlic will take only seconds, so watch it carefully.

6 Reheat the soup, then remove and discard curry leaves. Portion an equal amount of noodles among 4 serving bowls. Add equal amounts of chicken to each, then pour soup over the top. Top each bowl with half an egg and some of the fried noodles, onions, and garlic. Serve with cilantro and a lime wedge.

NOODLE SWAP // buckwheat flour noodles (see p36) // dried buckwheat soba noodles

BUCKWHEAT NOODLE SOUP WITH ENOKI & SHIITAKE

Making your own dashi, or Japanese stock, is a very simple affair that creates a delicate yet flavorful soup base. Here both dried and fresh shiitake are used to make a vegetarian version.

INGREDIENTS

1 batch of buckwheat flour dough (see p36), cut into spaghetti (see p44)

2oz (60g) fresh enoki mushrooms

4 scallions, finely sliced on the diagonal

8 small seaweed snack sheets (kim nori), cut into thin strips, to garnish

for the dashi

½oz (15g) dried kombu, cut into pieces

½oz (15g) dried shiitake mushrooms

2oz (60g) fresh shiitake mushrooms, stalks and caps separate, and caps thinly sliced

salt

1 tsp rice vinegar

1 tbsp soy sauce

serves 4 // time 15 mins, plus 1 to 3 hrs for soaking // gluten free // vegetarian

METHOD

1 To make the dashi: place dried kombu, dried shiitake mushrooms, and fresh shiitake mushroom stalks in a saucepan and cover with 5½ cups cold water. Soak for 1 to 3 hours.

2 After soaking, bring dashi nearly to a boil over medium heat, but remove from heat just before it boils. Season with salt, and stir in rice vinegar and soy sauce. Remove and discard kombu, and let dashi cool. Strain dashi through a sieve lined with paper towel to remove shiitake mushrooms.

3 Cook noodles in boiling, salted water for 3 to 4 minutes until just al dente. Drain and rinse well under cold water.

4 In a large saucepan, bring dashi to a boil over medium-high heat. Add enoki mushrooms, scallions, sliced shiitake mushroom caps, and noodles. Return to a boil until noodles are heated through and mushrooms are soft. Remove from heat and season to taste with salt. Serve immediately, topped with seaweed strips.

NOODLE SWAP // dried buckwheat soba noodles // dried millet noodles

HOT & SOUR SHIRATAKI SOUP WITH MUSHROOMS

Chili oil and lemongrass give this dish a sophisticated hot and sour flavor. Dark and distinctive cloud ear mushrooms have a mild taste and firm texture that holds up in the brothy soup.

INGREDIENTS

½ oz (15g) dried cloud ear mushrooms

2 tbsp rice wine vinegar

2 tbsp soy sauce

2 tsp chili oil

pinch of white pepper

2 tsp corn starch

1 tsp sugar

2 x 7oz (200g) packages shirataki noodles

8oz (225g) bamboo shoots, drained and julienned

for the soup base

6 cups good quality chicken stock

1 stalk lemongrass, roughly chopped

4 scallions, finely sliced, white and green parts kept separate

2 garlic cloves, bruised with the side of a knife

1-in (2.5cm) piece fresh ginger root, thinly sliced

¼ tsp red pepper flakes

serves 4 // time 1 hr // dairy free

METHOD

1 To make the soup base: in a medium saucepan, combine chicken stock, lemongrass, green parts of scallions, garlic, ginger, and red pepper flakes. Bring to a boil. Reduce to a simmer and cook, covered, for 15 minutes.

2 While soup base is simmering, place mushrooms in a heatproof bowl and cover with boiling water. Let soak for at least 15 minutes. Then drain, rinse well, and drain again before finely slicing for later use.

3 In a small bowl, mix together rice wine vinegar, soy sauce, chili oil, white pepper, corn starch, and sugar.

4 When soup base is ready, strain it, discard the solids, rinse the pan, and return the soup base to the pan. Bring to a boil and whisk in soy sauce mixture. Reduce to a very low simmer, add sliced mushrooms, and cook, covered, for 15 minutes until mushrooms soften but still retain some bite.

5 Drain shirataki noodles from the packaging liquid and rinse well under cold running water. Drain again and blot with paper towel to remove as much water as possible.

6 Add shirataki and bamboo shoots to the pan and cook for 2 minutes until heated through. Adjust seasoning, adding extra rice wine vinegar or chili oil if desired. Portion evenly among 4 serving bowls and top with white parts of scallions.

NOODLE SWAP // dried rice vermicelli // dried glass noodles // kelp noodles

COCONUT SHRIMP LAKSA

An aromatic spice blend of garlic, chilies, ginger, and lemongrass forms the flavorful base for this rich and spicy noodle soup, which has origins in Southeast Asia.

INGREDIENTS

2 tbsp coconut oil

13.5fl oz (400ml) can coconut milk

2 cups seafood stock

4 fresh or frozen lime leaves, roughly torn

5½oz (150g) dried glass noodles

8oz (225g) raw shrimp, peeled, de-veined, and halved lengthwise

1 tbsp lime juice

2 tsp fish sauce

¼ tsp sugar

1 tbsp finely chopped cilantro

2 scallions, finely sliced on the diagonal

1 lime, quartered, to serve

for the spice paste

2 stalks lemongrass, trimmed and tender parts finely chopped

1 red chile pepper, de-seeded and chopped

2 garlic cloves, chopped

1-in (2.5cm) piece fresh ginger root, peeled and chopped

1 tbsp roughly chopped cilantro stems

¼ red onion, roughly chopped

¼ cup sunflower oil

serves 4 // time 45 mins // dairy free // gluten free

METHOD

1 To make the spice paste: put all ingredients in the bowl of a food processor or high-powered blender and process until smooth. (The lemongrass can be tough to break down, so be sure to use only the tender inner parts.)

2 In a large, heavy-bottomed saucepan, heat coconut oil over low heat. Add spice paste and cook for 2 to 3 minutes until it darkens slightly and begins to separate.

3 Gradually stir in coconut milk, then add seafood stock and lime leaves and bring to a boil. Reduce to a simmer and cook, covered, for 10 minutes.

4 Meanwhile, place noodles in a large, heatproof bowl and cover with boiling water. Soak for 5 minutes, then drain, rinse under cold water, drain again, and set aside.

5 When broth is ready, remove lime leaves and discard. Add raw shrimp and cook over medium heat just until shrimp become pink and curl. Add lime juice, fish sauce, and sugar.

6 Portion equal amounts of noodles among 4 serving bowls. Add equal amounts of broth and shrimp to each. Top with cilantro and scallions and serve with a lime wedge alongside.

NOODLE SWAP // dried rice vermicelli // dried rice stick noodles

CHICKEN PHO WITH SWEET POTATO VERMICELLI

Leaving the chicken to cool in the broth ensures tender meat infused with the flavors of spices and aromatics. For added heat, garnish with thinly sliced red chiles or chili garlic sauce.

INGREDIENTS

4oz (115g) dried sweet potato vermicelli

for the soup base

2 whole chicken legs (thigh and drumstick), bone in and skin on

2 whole star anise

1 cinnamon stick

1 tsp coriander seeds

1 tsp black peppercorns

1 tsp salt

2 tsp light brown sugar

2 tbsp fish sauce, plus extra to serve

1 small onion, peeled and quartered

3-in (7.5cm) piece fresh ginger root, sliced

small handful of cilantro stems, roughly chopped

to serve

6oz (175g) bean sprouts

4 scallions, trimmed and finely shredded on the diagonal

large handful of cilantro leaves

large handful of mint leaves

large handful of Thai basil leaves

serves 4 // time 55 mins, plus 2 hrs for cooling // dairy free // gluten free

METHOD

1 To make the soup base: place chicken legs, skin-side up, in a large, heavy-bottomed pot with a lid. Cover with 7 cups water, and add all other ingredients. Bring to a boil, skimming off any foam that forms.

2 Reduce to a simmer and cook, covered, for 20 minutes. Turn off heat and let chicken cool in stock for about 2 hours, or until cool enough to handle.

3 Remove chicken and set aside to cool. Strain broth, discard the solids, wash the pot, and return broth to the pot. When chicken is cool, discard skin, remove meat from bones, and shred it with your fingers.

4 Place noodles in a heatproof bowl and add boiling water to cover. Soak for at least 15 minutes until soft. (Noodles can soak in the water until you are ready to serve the dish.)

5 Reheat broth until just boiling. Add shredded chicken and cook for another 1 to 2 minutes to reheat. Drain noodles and portion evenly among 4 bowls. Add equal amounts of broth and chicken to each bowl.

6 Serve immediately with a plate of bean sprouts, scallions, cilantro, mint, and Thai basil on the side, plus extra fish sauce, if desired.

NOODLE SWAP // dried rice vermicelli // dried glass noodles // kelp noodles

CALDO VERDE WITH QUINOA SPIRALS

This version of a traditional Portuguese soup is made with linguiça, a spicy cured and dried sausage. If it's difficult to find, replace it with chorizo or andouille instead.

INGREDIENTS

8oz (225g) dried quinoa rotini

4 tbsp olive oil, plus extra to toss

1 small yellow onion, finely chopped

3 garlic cloves, crushed

6oz (175g) linguiça sausage, about 3, casings removed and finely diced

6oz (175g) white potatoes, peeled, halved, and finely sliced

6½ cups good quality chicken or vegetable stock

salt and freshly ground black pepper

8oz (225g) de-ribbed and finely shredded kale

¼ tsp smoked paprika

serves 4–6 // time 50 mins // dairy free // gluten free

METHOD

1 Cook pasta according to the package instructions until just al dente. Drain, rinse well under cold water, and set aside. Once cool, toss with a drizzle of olive oil to prevent sticking.

2 In a large, heavy-bottomed saucepan, heat 3 tbsp olive oil over medium heat. Add onion and cook for 2 to 3 minutes until soft but not brown.

3 Add garlic and linguiça, and cook for 2 to 3 minutes until oil is released from sausage. Then stir in potatoes.

4 Add chicken stock and bring to a boil. Season with black pepper and a little salt to taste. Reduce heat, cover, and simmer for at least 20 minutes until potatoes are completely cooked through and beginning to break down.

5 Using a potato masher, mash potatoes in the soup until the soup is smooth and thickened. Add kale and continue to cook for another 5 minutes until kale is soft. Add pasta and cook for 1 to 2 minutes until heated through.

6 In a small saucepan, heat remaining 1 tbsp olive oil. Remove from heat and stir in paprika. Portion equal amounts of soup into bowls, add a swirl of spicy paprika oil to the top of each, and serve immediately.

PASTA SWAP // dried einkorn rotini // dried red lentil rotini

PASTA
SALADS

THAI NOODLE SALAD WITH PAPAYA & LOTUS ROOT

Making your own quick pickles is easy, and their refreshing, sharp flavors can really finish a dish. Lotus root is beautiful, but normal radishes work just as well.

INGREDIENTS

8oz (225g) dried glass noodles

8oz (225g) green papaya or green mango, julienned

2 carrots, julienned

½ small red onion, very finely sliced

2 under-ripe tomatoes, halved and cut into very thin wedges

2 tbsp dried shrimp, very finely chopped or crushed with a mortar and pestle

handful of mint leaves, roughly chopped

handful of cilantro leaves, roughly chopped

2 tbsp salted peanuts, roughly chopped

for the pickled lotus

1 lotus root, peeled and thinly sliced, about 3½oz (100g) in total

½ cup rice wine vinegar

¼ cup sugar

1 tsp fine sea salt

for the dressing

4 tsp sugar

4 tbsp lime juice

2 tbsp fish sauce

2 tbsp rice wine vinegar

1 garlic clove, crushed

serves 6 // time 30 mins, plus 24 hrs for pickling // dairy free

METHOD

1 To make the pickled lotus: soak sliced lotus root in cold water for 20 to 30 minutes. Drain, then blanch in boiling water for 1 to 2 minutes. Drain and refresh under cold water then stack the slices in a small glass jar. Whisk together rice wine vinegar, sugar, and salt until sugar has dissolved. Pour vinegar mixture over lotus root, cover, and refrigerate for at least 1 day and up to 5 days before using.

2 To make the dressing: whisk together all ingredients, along with 2 tbsp water, until sugar has dissolved.

3 Place noodles in a heatproof bowl and cover with boiling water. Soak for 15 minutes until soft, and snip with kitchen scissors to make a more manageable length to eat. Drain, rinse well under cold water, and set aside to cool and drain completely.

4 In a large bowl, combine cooled noodles with finely sliced vegetables, dried shrimp, and most of the chopped herbs and peanuts. Add dressing and toss very well until dressing is completely incorporated.

5 Heap salad into the middle of a serving bowl and scatter with reserved herbs and peanuts. Top with pickled lotus root and serve immediately with any extra dressing and lotus root on the side.

NOODLE SWAP // dried rice vermicelli // shirataki noodles

RAINBOW BOWL WITH SESAME & GINGER DRESSING

To maximize the visual impact of the colorful, fresh ingredients, serve this salad with the vegetables displayed in sections and the dressing in a bowl alongside ready to toss at the table.

serves 4 // time 10 mins // dairy free // vegetarian

INGREDIENTS

2 thick carrots, trimmed and peeled

1 medium beet, peeled

½ English cucumber, trimmed

2 small summer squash or
 yellow carrots, trimmed

1 tsp black sesame seeds, to garnish

cilantro leaves, to garnish

lime halves, to serve

for the dressing

2 tbsp sunflower oil

2 tbsp lime juice

2 tsp sesame oil

2 tsp soy sauce

2 tsp honey

1 garlic clove, crushed

1-in (2.5cm) piece fresh ginger root,
 peeled and finely grated

½ small shallot, minced

METHOD

1 To make the dressing: whisk all ingredients together. For a more emulsified finish, blend them in a small blender or food processor.

2 Spiralize carrots, beet, cucumber, and squash. Portion spiralized vegetables evenly among 4 bowls, laying out the vegetables in contrasting piles. Scatter each serving with sesame seeds and cilantro. Serve with dressing and lime halves alongside.

SHIRATAKI & SHRIMP SUMMER ROLLS

These light and tasty rolls are stuffed with shirataki noodles, shrimp, and fresh herbs, but they can take a variety of fillings. Use vibrant, crisp vegetables and mix and match as you prefer.

INGREDIENTS

8 x 6-in (15cm) rice paper wrappers

16 large, cooked shrimp, halved horizontally

small handful of cilantro leaves

small handful of mint leaves

small handful of Thai basil leaves

2 x 7oz (200g) packages shirataki noodles, drained, rinsed, and dried

1 large carrot, julienned

4 scallions, julienned

small handful of pea shoots

for the dipping sauce

2 tbsp sugar

1½ tbsp fish sauce

1 tbsp rice wine vinegar

juice of 1 lime

½ garlic clove, crushed

pinch of red pepper flakes

makes 8 rolls // time 30 mins // dairy free // gluten free

METHOD

1 To make the dipping sauce: in a small saucepan, heat sugar and 2 tbsp water over medium heat, whisking frequently, until sugar has dissolved. Remove from heat and let cool. Then add remaining ingredients and whisk to combine.

2 Fill a large bowl with warm water. Fully submerge 1 rice paper wrapper for 10 to 15 seconds until it just starts to soften. Shake any excess water from it, and lay it flat on a clean work surface.

3 Take 2 shrimp halves and lay them pink-side down along the center of wrapper. Top the shrimp with a few leaves of mint, basil, and cilantro. Then add a little of the shirataki noodles, a few julienned carrots and scallions, and a few pea shoots, leaving the edges of the wrapper free. Finish with 2 more shrimp halves, pink-side up.

4 The wrapper should be fully softened and pliable by now, but not too delicate. Wrap the nearest side to you up over filling, tuck outside edges up over filling, and roll wrapper away from you, tucking as you go, to fully encase filling. Place on a plate, cover with a damp paper towel, and refrigerate. Repeat steps 2 to 4 to make all 8 rolls, continuing to chill them as you go.

5 After assembling all 8 rolls, serve immediately with dipping sauce on the side.

NOODLE SWAP // dried glass noodles // dried rice vermicelli // kelp noodles

TZATZIKI CUCUMBER NOODLE SALAD

Dressed with the sharp, fresh flavors of yogurt, garlic, and mint, this salad of spiralized cucumber makes an excellent accompaniment to herby grilled lamb or quick-broiled salmon.

INGREDIENTS

2 English cucumbers, spiralized

½ tsp salt

1 cup Greek yogurt

2 garlic cloves, crushed

2 tsp white vinegar

1 tbsp olive oil

handful of mint leaves, finely chopped, plus extra to garnish

1 tbsp finely chopped dill, plus extra to garnish

zest of ½ small lemon

salt and freshly ground black pepper

serves 4 // time 15 mins, plus 1 hr for chilling // gluten free // vegetarian

METHOD

1 Place spiralized cucumbers in a large sieve and toss with salt. Set the sieve over a bowl, place in the refrigerator, and let drain for 1 hour.

2 While cucumbers drain, stir garlic into yogurt, cover, and refrigerate.

3 Rinse drained cucumbers briefly under cold water and gently squeeze dry, then place in a clean dish towel and wring as much extra water as possible from them. Place in a large mixing bowl and snip with kitchen scissors to make a more manageable length to eat.

4 Add vinegar, olive oil, mint, dill, and lemon zest to yogurt, and season with pepper. Mix yogurt into cucumber noodles. Taste and adjust seasoning as needed. Place in a serving dish. Garnish with extra mint and dill, and serve immediately.

NOODLE SWAP // spiralized zucchini

PICKLED VEGETABLE SALAD WITH SHIRATAKI & SEAWEED

Taking its inspiration from the ubiquitous Japanese seaweed salad, here shirataki noodles are tossed with pickled radish, carrot, cucumber, and onion to make a more substantial dish.

INGREDIENTS

1 tbsp hijiki seaweed

2 x 7oz (200g) packages shirataki noodles

nori furikake, to serve

for the pickled vegetables

½ cup rice wine vinegar

¼ cup white sugar

1 tsp fine salt

1 garlic clove, crushed

1 tsp finely grated ginger

4 radishes, julienned

2 carrots, julienned

¼ small red onion, finely sliced

4-in (10cm) piece cucumber, de-seeded and julienned

2-in (5cm) piece daikon radish, julienned

serves 4 // time 35 mins, plus 1 hr for pickling // dairy free // gluten free

METHOD

1 To make the pickled vegetables: in a small bowl, whisk together rice wine vinegar, sugar, salt, garlic, and ginger until sugar and salt have dissolved. In a large bowl, toss radishes, carrots, red onion, cucumber, and daikon, and add pickling liquid. Cover and chill, turning occasionally, for at least 1 hour.

2 Place hijiki in a small, heatproof bowl and cover with boiling water. Soak for 10 minutes, or until soft, then drain, refresh under cold water, and drain again. Blot with paper towel to remove excess water. Set aside.

3 Bring a pot of water to a boil over high heat. Drain shirataki noodles of the packaging liquid, and rinse well under cold water. Plunge them briefly into the boiling water, then drain again, rinse under cold water, and blot with paper towel to remove as much water as possible. Snip with kitchen scissors to make a more manageable length to eat.

4 When vegetables are lightly pickled, add shirataki noodles and hijiki to the bowl and toss well to combine. Transfer to a serving bowl (leaving behind excess pickling liquid) and top with a sprinkle of furikake before serving.

NOODLE SWAP // dried glass noodles // kelp noodles

VIETNAMESE CHICKEN NOODLE SALAD

Based on the traditional Vietnamese dish of "bún," this refreshing noodle salad is tossed in a zesty citrus dressing and topped with chicken flavored with ginger and lemongrass.

INGREDIENTS

4 large skinless, boneless chicken thighs

10oz (300g) dried rice vermicelli

1 heart of romaine lettuce, trimmed and shredded

¼ English cucumber, spiralized

1 large, thick carrot, spiralized

2 large handfuls of bean sprouts

4 scallions, finely sliced

handful of mint leaves, lightly chopped

handful of Thai basil, lightly chopped

2 heaped tbsp salted peanuts, roughly chopped

for the marinade

1 large or 2 small stalks lemongrass, peeled, trimmed, and finely chopped

½-in (1.5cm) piece fresh ginger root, peeled and roughly chopped

1 garlic clove, roughly chopped

1 tbsp roughly chopped cilantro stems

2 tbsp sunflower oil

1 tbsp lime juice

2 tsp light brown sugar

2 tsp soy sauce

2 tsp fish sauce

for the dressing

4 tbsp lemon juice

4 tsp fish sauce

3 tsp sugar

1 garlic clove, crushed

pinch of white pepper

serves 4 // time 1 hr, plus 2 hrs for marinating // dairy free

METHOD

1 To make the marinade: place all ingredients in the bowl of a food processor and process until smooth.

2 With a rolling pin or meat mallet, pound chicken thighs to flatten them to even thicknesses. Place in a shallow dish and add marinade. Using your hands, rub marinade into chicken. Refrigerate, covered, for at least 2 hours and up to 12 hours.

3 To make the dressing: whisk together all ingredients until sugar has dissolved. Then whisk in 4 tbsp cold water and set aside.

4 Place noodles in a large, heatproof bowl and cover with boiling water. Let soak for 15 minutes until soft. Drain, rinse well under cold water, and drain again. Set aside to cool and drain completely.

5 Preheat the broiler to high. Line a large, rimmed baking sheet with aluminum foil and arrange marinated chicken in a single layer. Broil chicken for 5 to 7 minutes on each side until dark brown and crispy in places. Set aside to cool slightly.

6 Portion lettuce evenly among 4 bowls and top each bowl with an equal amount of noodles, spiralized cucumber and carrot, and bean sprouts. Lightly toss the ingredients in each bowl.

7 Top each bowl with 1 chicken thigh, sliced on the diagonal. Sprinkle with scallions, mint, Thai basil, and peanuts. Serve immediately with dressing on the side.

NOODLE SWAP // dried glass noodles // shirataki noodles

RED LENTIL ROTINI WITH OLIVES & ANCHOVIES

Blending citrus and fresh basil with olive oil creates a bright, bold dressing to coat this earthy pasta, which loses its red hue when cooked. The Castelvetrano olives lend an irresistible buttery-sweet flavor.

serves 4 // time 20 mins // dairy free // gluten free

METHOD

1 Cook pasta according to the package instructions until just al dente. Drain, rinse well under cold water, and set aside to drain and cool completely.

2 To make the dressing: in a blender or food processor, combine olive oil, anchovies, lemon zest, lemon juice, and basil leaves. Season well with pepper and a little salt. Blend until fully emulsified with only small flecks of basil. Taste and adjust seasoning as desired.

3 In a large bowl, toss the cooled pasta with dressing until well coated. Add olives and capers, and toss again. Garnish with basil and serve immediately.

INGREDIENTS

14oz (400g) dried red lentil rotini
12 green Castelvetrano olives, pitted and thinly sliced lengthwise
2 tbsp capers, finely chopped

for the dressing

1 cup olive oil
2oz (56g) tin anchovies
zest of 1 large or 2 small lemons
1 tbsp lemon juice
2oz (60g) basil leaves, plus extra to garnish
salt and freshly ground black pepper

PASTA SWAP // dried green lentil shells // dried chickpea rotini

GREEN TEA SOBA WITH SESAME-CRUSTED TUNA

This cool and refreshing salad can be a tasty starter or light main course. To make vegan, top with grilled mushrooms instead of tuna. To make gluten free, replace soy sauce with liquid aminos.

INGREDIENTS

10oz (300g) dried green tea soba noodles

2 tbsp hijiki dried seaweed, soaked and drained

4-in (10cm) piece cucumber, quartered lengthwise, de-seeded, and julienned

4oz (115g) enoki mushrooms

4 scallions, julienned

4 tbsp mixed black and white sesame seeds

4 x 6oz (175g) tuna steaks

2 tbsp sunflower oil

salt and freshly ground black pepper

for the dressing

3 tbsp mirin

2 tbsp soy sauce

2 tsp sesame oil

1 tsp sugar

serves 4 // time 25 mins, plus 30 mins to chill // dairy free

METHOD

1 Cook noodles according to the package instructions until just al dente. Drain and rinse well under cold water until cool. Let dry, blotting with paper towel if necessary.

2 To make the dressing: in a large bowl, whisk together all ingredients until sugar has dissolved.

3 Add noodles, hijiki, cucumber, enoki, and most of sliced scallions to the bowl with dressing. Toss well to combine, then chill for at least 30 minutes.

4 Place most of sesame seeds on a small plate. Brush the outer edges of tuna steaks with a little sunflower oil, season well with salt and pepper, and roll to coat the edges in sesame seeds. In a large, non-stick frying pan, heat sunflower oil over medium heat. Put tuna in the pan and cook for 2 to 3 minutes on each side until medium rare, depending on the thickness of the pieces.

5 To serve, portion dressed noodles among 4 shallow bowls, tossing with a little extra soy sauce and sesame oil if desired. Top each bowl with 1 tuna steak, sliced, and garnish with remaining scallions and sesame seeds. Serve immediately with extra soy sauce on the side.

NOODLE SWAP // buckwheat flour spaghetti (see p36) // dried buckwheat soba noodles

QUINOA SHELLS WITH BURRATA, BASIL & TOMATO

In the heat of the summer, when tomatoes are at their most plentiful and flavorsome, this no-cook sauce of tomato, basil, and garlic makes a quick midweek meal.

INGREDIENTS

8oz (225g) dried quinoa shells

6 Roma tomatoes

1 garlic clove, crushed

3 tbsp olive oil, plus extra to toss

handful of basil leaves, plus extra to garnish

salt and freshly ground black pepper

4oz (115g) burrata, roughly torn

¼ tsp lemon zest

serves 4 // time 25 mins // gluten free // vegetarian

METHOD

1 Cook pasta according to the package instructions until just al dente. Drain, then rinse under cold water. Drain again, toss with a drizzle of olive oil to prevent sticking, and set aside to cool.

2 Make several small cuts in the skin of each tomato and place in a heatproof bowl. Cover with boiling water and let stand for 1 minute. Drain the water. Once cool enough to handle, skin tomatoes (the skin will start to peel away where it has been cut). Halve them, squeeze out and discard any excess juice and most of the seeds, then roughly chop and put in a food processor.

3 Add garlic, olive oil, and basil to the food processor, and season very well. Process to a rough sauce. Test for seasoning.

4 To assemble salad: mix together cooled pasta, tomato sauce, and most of torn burrata. Pile into a serving bowl and top with remaining burrata, lemon zest, and a few torn basil leaves. Serve immediately.

PASTA SWAP // corn flour orecchiette (see p38) // dried brown rice shells // dried corn shells

PEANUT SHIRATAKI SALAD WITH CHILI OIL

The peanut dressing that coats this tangle of noodles and crisp vegetables is mouthwatering—make it spicier with extra chili oil or sharper with more lime juice, as you prefer.

INGREDIENTS

2 x 7oz (200g) packages shirataki noodles
¼ red pepper, de-seeded and julienned
1 large carrot, julienned
2oz (60g) white cabbage, julienned
¼ small red onion, very finely sliced
handful of cilantro leaves, chopped
handful of Thai basil, chopped
2 tbsp salted peanuts, roughly chopped

for the dressing

1oz (30g) creamy peanut butter
1 tbsp lime juice
1 tbsp rice wine vinegar
½ tbsp soy sauce
½ tbsp sesame oil
1 garlic clove, roughly chopped
1-in (2.5cm) piece fresh ginger root, roughly chopped
½ tsp chili oil
pinch of sugar

serves 4–6 // time 35 mins // dairy free // vegetarian

METHOD

1 Bring a pot of water to a boil over high heat. Drain shirataki noodles of the packaging liquid, and rinse well under cold water. Plunge them briefly into the boiling water, then drain again, rinse under cold water, and blot with paper towel to remove as much water as possible.

2 To make the dressing: put all ingredients in a small blender along with 2 tbsp cold water and blend until smooth. Set aside. If you do not have a blender small enough to crush garlic and ginger, these can be finely grated and whisked with the other ingredients until well combined.

3 Put noodles in a large bowl. Snip with kitchen scissors to make a more manageable length to eat. Toss them in dressing. Add red pepper, carrot, cabbage, onion, cilantro, basil, and peanuts, reserving some of the cilantro, basil, and peanuts for garnish. Pile salad into a serving bowl and top with reserved herbs and peanuts. Serve immediately.

NOODLE SWAP // dried rice vermicelli // dried rice stick noodles

KELP NOODLE SALAD WITH CITRUS & SHRIMP

Mint and cilantro bring a fresh, herbal flavor to this cool and refreshing salad, which is dressed with a piquant blend of citrus juices and topped with tender shrimp and crisp vegetables.

INGREDIENTS

10oz (300g) kelp noodles

2oz (60g) white cabbage, finely shredded

2oz (60g) sugar snap peas, trimmed and finely sliced lengthwise

handful of pea shoots

handful of baby arugula

2oz (60g) red onion, very finely sliced

8oz (225g) cooked shrimp, sliced in half lengthwise

2 tbsp roughly chopped cilantro leaves

2 tbsp roughly chopped mint leaves

for the dressing

4 tbsp orange juice

2 tbsp lemon juice

2 tbsp lime juice

2 tsp rice wine vinegar

2 tsp fish sauce

1 tsp sugar

serves 4 // time 40 mins // dairy free // gluten free

METHOD

1 Rinse kelp noodles under cold, running water for at least 30 seconds. Place in a heatproof bowl and cover with boiling water. Let soak for 30 minutes, then drain and rinse once more under cold water to cool. Drain, then dry completely with paper towel. Snip with kitchen scissors to make a more manageable length to eat.

2 To make the dressing: in a small bowl, whisk together all ingredients until sugar has dissolved.

3 In a large bowl, add kelp noodles and most of dressing. Use your hands to massage dressing into noodles to help soften them.

4 Add cabbage, snap peas, pea shoots, arugula, and red onion to noodles, and toss well to combine. Top with shrimp, cilantro, and mint, and lightly toss again. Serve immediately with remaining dressing on the side.

NOODLE SWAP // shirataki noodles // dried rice vermicelli // dried glass noodles

CAESAR PASTA SALAD WITH ANCHOVY CROUTONS

Sturdy einkorn rotini has a rustic texture that is well suited to absorb and carry all the strong, sharp flavors of the Caesar dressing.

INGREDIENTS

10oz (300g) dried einkorn rotini

olive oil, to toss

4oz (115g) hearts of romaine lettuce, trimmed of outer leaves and chopped

1oz (30g) Parmesan cheese, shaved, to serve

for the croutons

4oz (115g) day-old baguette

oil from 2oz (56g) tin anchovies

salt and freshly ground black pepper

for the dressing

2 egg yolks

4 anchovy fillets

1½ tbsp lemon juice

1 tsp Dijon mustard

1 garlic clove, crushed

2 tbsp grated Parmesan cheese

½ cup olive oil

½ cup sunflower oil

serves 4 // time 30 mins

METHOD

1 Preheat the oven to 375°F (190°C). To make the croutons: cut baguette into large pieces, then process briefly in a food processor to make small, irregular pieces. In a small bowl, toss bread with the anchovy oil until well coated, adding a little extra olive oil if needed. Season well with salt and pepper, and spread in a single layer on a large baking sheet. Bake on the top rack of the oven for 5 to 7 minutes, turning occasionally, until golden brown. Remove from the oven and set aside.

2 To make the dressing: in a food processor, combine egg yolks, anchovies, lemon juice, Dijon mustard, garlic, and Parmesan. Season well with pepper. Process until fairly smooth, then add olive oil and sunflower oil with the machine on, in a very thin stream, until dressing emulsifies and is thick and smooth.

3 Cook pasta according to the package instructions until just al dente. Drain, rinse under cold water, and drain again. Toss with a drizzle of olive oil to prevent sticking, and let cool completely.

4 In a large bowl, toss together cooled pasta and most of dressing. Add lettuce and most of croutons and toss again to combine. Serve immediately with Parmesan on top, and remaining dressing and croutons on the side.

PASTA SWAP // spelt & chestnut flour farfalle (see p42) // dried spelt rotini // dried rye trumpets

BUCKWHEAT NOODLES WITH SOY, MAPLE & CHILI SAUCE

Nutty buckwheat noodles and crisp daikon are tossed with a sweet and spicy sauce that gets its heat from gochujang, a Korean chili paste. Ginger, garlic, and sesame round out the flavors of the dish.

INGREDIENTS

12oz (350g) dried 100% buckwheat noodles

salt

sesame oil, to toss

4–6 scallions, finely sliced on the diagonal

3-in (7.5cm) piece daikon radish, peeled and finely julienned

1 tbsp furikake, to garnish

for the dressing

4 tbsp sunflower oil

2 tbsp rice wine vinegar

1 tsp gochujang paste

1 tbsp sesame oil

1 tbsp maple syrup

1 tbsp soy sauce

1 garlic clove, crushed

½-in (1cm) piece fresh ginger root, peeled and roughly grated

serves **4** // time **20 mins** // **dairy free**

METHOD

1 Cook noodles according to the package instructions in boiling, salted water until just al dente. Drain, rinse well under cold water, and drain again. Toss with a drizzle of sesame oil to prevent sticking, and set aside to cool.

2 To make the dressing: in a medium bowl, combine all ingredients and whisk until smooth.

3 In a large bowl, combine noodles, scallions, daikon, and dressing. Toss until well combined and evenly coated in sauce. Transfer salad to a serving bowl and sprinkle with furikake. Serve immediately.

NOODLE SWAP // dried oat flour noodles // buckwheat flour noodles (see p36)

LENTIL PASTA SALAD WITH CHICKPEAS & PRESERVED LEMON

This hearty side dish is bursting with Mediterranean flavors. Fresh basil and feta top the lentil pasta and chickpeas, which soak up the piquant saltiness of the preserved lemon dressing.

INGREDIENTS

4oz (115g) dried chickpeas, soaked overnight

8oz (225g) dried green lentil shells

olive oil, to toss

10oz (300g) yellow cherry tomatoes, quartered

4oz (115g) feta cheese, crumbled

for the dressing

¼ cup olive oil

2 tbsp finely chopped preserved lemon (rinse well before chopping)

1 garlic clove, crushed

½ tsp sugar

1 tbsp lemon juice

handful of basil leaves, plus extra to serve

salt and freshly ground black pepper

serves 8 // time 1 hr 10 mins, plus overnight to soak // gluten free // vegetarian

METHOD

1 In a medium saucepan, cover chickpeas with cold water and bring to a boil over high heat. Skim off any foam, then reduce to a simmer and cook, uncovered, for 45 minutes to 1 hour until soft. Drain and rinse under cold water. Set aside to cool.

2 Meanwhile, cook pasta according to the package instructions until just al dente. Drain, rinse under cold water, and drain again. Toss with a drizzle of olive oil to prevent sticking, and set aside to cool.

3 While pasta and chickpeas cool, make the dressing: place all ingredients in a blender or small food processor and season well. Add 2 tbsp cold water and blend until smooth.

4 To assemble: toss pasta, chickpeas, cherry tomatoes, and most of feta together with dressing until well combined. Transfer to a serving bowl and scatter with remaining feta and a few basil leaves, roughly torn. Serve immediately.

PASTA SWAP // dried red lentil rotini // dried quinoa penne

SPICY TAHINI BLACK RICE NOODLE SALAD

This stunning salad is tasty on its own as a light lunch or side dish, or topped with grilled salmon teriyaki as a main dish. Caramelized pumpkin seeds add a sweet and spicy crunch.

INGREDIENTS

10oz (300g) dried black rice noodles

sunflower oil, to toss

2 large carrots, peeled

7oz (200g) red cabbage, very finely sliced

4 scallions, julienned

handful of cilantro leaves, finely chopped

salt and freshly ground black pepper

for the pumpkin seeds

1 tsp sunflower oil

1 tbsp light brown sugar

pinch of salt

pinch of chili powder

2oz (60g) raw shelled pumpkin seeds

for the dressing

2 tbsp tahini

2 tbsp sunflower oil

1 tsp chili oil

2 tbsp lime juice

1 tbsp soy sauce

1 tbsp honey

serves 4–6 // time 30 mins // dairy free // vegetarian

METHOD

1 Preheat the oven to 350°F (180°C) and line a baking sheet with parchment paper. To make the caramelized pumpkin seeds: in a small bowl, whisk together sunflower oil, sugar, salt, and chili powder. Add pumpkin seeds and toss to thoroughly coat, then spread on prepared baking sheet. Bake on the top rack of the oven for 5 to 7 minutes, until seeds begin to brown and stick together. Remove from the oven and spread on a plate to cool. Once cool, break up any clumps.

2 To make the dressing: whisk together all ingredients along with 2 tbsp cold water until completely emulsified. Set aside.

3 Cook noodles according to the package instructions. Then drain, rinse well under cold water, and drain again. Toss with a drizzle of sunflower oil to prevent sticking. Let cool completely.

4 Use a potato peeler to peel wide ribbons of carrot into a serving bowl. Add cabbage, scallions, and most of pumpkin seeds and cilantro, along with cooled noodles. Add dressing and toss well to combine.

5 Heap salad in the center of the serving bowl. Sprinkle with reserved pumpkin seeds and cilantro. Season with salt and pepper to taste, and serve immediately.

NOODLE SWAP // dried buckwheat soba noodles // dried rice stick noodles

SUMMER SQUASH SALAD WITH OLIVES & FETA

This is best served cold as a side dish, so chill the squash before you start. The salty olives and feta combine with the tangy dressing, making a light lunch. Add poached shrimp for a fuller meal.

INGREDIENTS

2 small zucchini

2 small yellow summer squash

2 tbsp very finely diced red onion

4oz (115g) feta cheese, roughly crumbled

16 pitted Kalamata olives, blotted dry and cut into quarters lengthwise

for the dressing

4 tbsp buttermilk

4 tbsp olive oil

2 tbsp lemon juice

salt and freshly ground black pepper

pinch of sugar

handful of mint leaves, finely chopped, plus a few whole leaves to garnish

serves 4 // time 10 mins // gluten free // vegetarian

METHOD

1 To make the dressing: in a small bowl, whisk together all ingredients until emulsified.

2 Spiralize zucchini and squash using a fine blade and removing the core. Once cut, spread them out in a thin layer on paper towel and blot well to remove as much moisture as possible.

3 In a serving bowl, combine spiralized vegetables, onion, and most of feta. Toss well.

4 Heap salad into the center of the serving bowl and scatter with remaining feta, sliced olives, and a few mint leaves. Serve immediately with dressing on the side.

PASTA
BOWLS

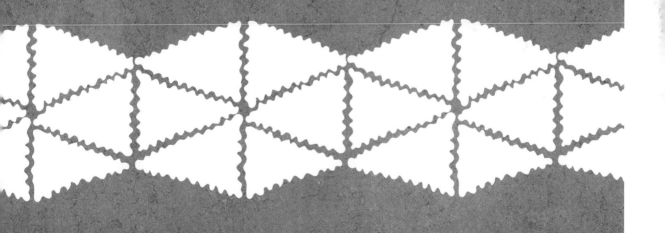

SPICY TURKEY & BUCKWHEAT NOODLE STIR-FRY

Gochujang, a sweet and spicy Korean chili paste, gives this dish a fiery heat as well as a rich flavor that complements the earthy buckwheat noodles.

serves 4 // time 1 hr // dairy free

INGREDIENTS

8oz (225g) dried 100% buckwheat noodles

1 tsp sesame oil, plus extra to toss

2 tbsp sunflower oil

10oz (300g) ground turkey

2-in (5cm) piece fresh ginger root, peeled and finely grated

2 garlic cloves, crushed

1 tbsp soy sauce

4oz (115g) green beans, trimmed and finely sliced on the diagonal

4oz (115g) asparagus spears, trimmed and finely sliced on the diagonal

2oz (60g) small broccoli florets, thinly cut

2oz (60g) sugar snap peas, trimmed and sliced in half diagonally

4 scallions, trimmed and finely sliced on the diagonal

handful of cilantro leaves, roughly chopped

for the sauce

1 tbsp gochujang paste

1 tbsp soy sauce

1 tbsp mirin

1 tsp sugar

1 tsp sesame oil

METHOD

1 To make the sauce: in a small bowl, whisk together all ingredients, along with 1 tbsp water. Set aside.

2 Cook noodles according to the package instructions until just al dente. Drain and rinse under cold water. Toss with a drizzle of sesame oil to prevent sticking. Set aside.

3 In a wok, heat sesame oil and 1 tbsp sunflower oil over high heat. When hot, add ground turkey and cook for 3 to 4 minutes, stirring constantly, until browned. Add ginger and garlic and cook for another 1 to 2 minutes until any liquid has evaporated. Stir in soy sauce. Remove from heat, transfer contents to a plate, and wipe out the wok with a paper towel.

4 In the wok, heat the remaining 1 tbsp sunflower oil over high heat. Add green beans and stir-fry for 1 minute. Add asparagus, broccoli, and sugar snap peas, and stir-fry for another 2 minutes until tender. Add 1 tbsp water to the wok if necessary to help vegetables cook through.

5 Add cooked noodles, sauce, and turkey to the wok. Toss well. Cook for a final 2 to 3 minutes until sauce comes together and noodles are heated through.

6 Add scallions and cilantro, reserving some of each for garnish, and toss briefly. Transfer to a serving dish and serve immediately, garnished with reserved scallions and cilantro.

NOODLE SWAP // buckwheat flour spaghetti (see p36) // dried einkorn spaghetti

CHICKPEA CACIO E PEPE WITH CRISPED LEEKS

Salty Parmesan and fiery red pepper flakes flavor this tangle of simple chickpea pasta. Crisped leeks provide a beautiful finish to the dish, as well as contrasting texture.

INGREDIENTS

salt and freshly ground black pepper

1 batch of chickpea flour dough (see p34), cut into spaghetti (see p44)

4 tbsp olive oil

4 tbsp butter

1 tsp freshly ground black pepper

1 tsp red pepper flakes, plus extra to serve

2oz (60g) Parmesan cheese, finely grated, plus extra to serve

for the crisped leeks

sunflower oil, for frying

2 leeks, washed and trimmed

1 tbsp cornstarch

salt

serves 4 // time 25 mins // gluten free

METHOD

1 To make the crisped leeks: in a medium, heavy-bottomed saucepan, pour in sunflower oil to a depth of 2in (5cm). Heat oil to 350°F (180°C). Meanwhile, slice leeks in half lengthwise, then very finely slice into thin strips. Blot away any moisture with paper towel. Toss leeks in cornstarch. When oil reaches temperature, working in batches, transfer leeks to the pan and fry until golden brown and crispy. Remove and place on paper towel to absorb oil. Season with salt to taste.

2 In a pot of boiling, salted water, cook pasta until al dente, about 4 minutes. Drain and reserve 1 cup cooking water.

3 In the same pot, heat olive oil, 2 tbsp butter, black pepper, and red pepper flakes over medium heat. Cook for 1 minute, or until fragrant. Add reserved cooking water, pasta, remaining 2 tbsp butter, and Parmesan. Toss until Parmesan melts in and water is absorbed, adding a little more water as desired. Taste and season with salt and pepper.

4 Serve immediately topped with crisped leeks, Parmesan, and a sprinkle of red pepper flakes.

PASTA SWAP // dried chickpea spaghetti **//** dried quinoa spaghetti

SPELT SPAGHETTI WITH RICOTTA & ARTICHOKE

Spelt pasta has a pleasant, mildly nutty taste that is paired with creamy ricotta in this light yet indulgent meal. The lemon and chili complement the delicate flavor of the grilled artichoke.

INGREDIENTS

14oz (400g) dried spelt spaghetti

12oz (340g) jar artichoke halves, marinated in oil

7oz (200g) ricotta cheese

2 tbsp olive oil

zest of 1 large lemon

1 tsp red pepper flakes

salt and freshly ground black pepper

*handful of basil leaves, finely chopped, plus a few
  whole leaves to garnish*

Parmesan cheese, shaved, to serve

serves 4 // time 30 mins

METHOD

1 Cook pasta according to the package instructions until just al dente. Drain, reserving ½ cup cooking water, and rinse pasta under cold water. Return pasta to the pot.

2 Meanwhile, remove artichokes from the jar and pat off oil with a paper towel. Heat a cast-iron griddle over medium-high heat. When hot, add artichokes and cook for 2 to 3 minutes per side until well browned with grill marks on them. Set aside to cool, then roughly slice lengthwise.

3 In a large bowl, whisk together ricotta, olive oil, lemon zest, and red pepper flakes. Season with salt and pepper. Add reserved cooking water to ricotta mixture and whisk until it forms a thick, smooth sauce.

4 In the pot, toss together sauce, basil, pasta, and artichokes. Taste and season with salt and pepper. Serve immediately, topped generously with shaved Parmesan and basil leaves.

PASTA SWAP // buckwheat flour spaghetti (see p36) // dried 100% buckwheat noodles

KOREAN STIR-FRIED GLASS NOODLES

This version of the classic Korean dish japchae is simple and quick to prepare. Boost the flavors of the dish by adding more garlic, grated ginger, or finely chopped fresh chilies, as desired.

INGREDIENTS

7oz (200g) skirt steak, thinly sliced

5½oz (150g) dried glass noodles

sesame oil, to toss

2 tbsp sunflower oil

4oz (115g) shiitake mushrooms, stems removed and finely sliced

½ small red onion, finely sliced

1 large carrot, julienned

¼ large red pepper, julienned

1oz (30g) baby spinach leaves

2 tbsp chicken stock

1 tbsp toasted sesame seeds, to garnish

2 scallions, finely sliced, to garnish

for the marinade

2 tbsp soy sauce

1 garlic clove, crushed

1 tsp sesame oil

1 tsp sugar

⅛ tsp white pepper

serves 2 // time **30 mins** // **dairy free**

METHOD

1 To make the marinade: in a medium bowl, whisk together all ingredients. Add steak and turn to coat. Cover with plastic wrap and refrigerate for at least 30 minutes until needed.

2 Place noodles in a large, heatproof bowl and cover with boiling water. Soak for 5 minutes, then snip with kitchen scissors to make a more manageable length to eat. Drain, rinse under cold water, and drain again. Toss with a drizzle of sesame oil to prevent sticking, then set aside to cool.

3 When steak is ready, heat 1 tbsp sunflower oil in a large wok. Add shiitake mushrooms and cook for 2 minutes, or until soft. Remove steak from marinade (retaining the liquid) and add it to the pan. Stir-fry for 2 minutes until steak is just cooked. Remove steak and mushrooms from the pan.

4 Heat remaining 1 tbsp sunflower oil in the wok and add onion, carrot, and red pepper. Stir-fry for 2 minutes, until just softened. Add glass noodles, along with remaining marinade, spinach, and chicken stock. Stir-fry for 1 minute until spinach wilts, then add steak and mushroom mixture, and cook for 1 minute more until heated through. Garnish with sesame seeds and scallions and serve immediately.

NOODLE SWAP // dried rice vermicelli // dried sweet potato vermicelli // shirataki noodles

RED LENTIL ROTINI WITH RED PEPPER & GARLIC SAUCE

Lentil pasta has a slightly peppery taste that works well with the robust flavors of this roasted red pepper and tomato sauce. Fresh basil and a sprinkle of Parmesan complete the dish.

INGREDIENTS

2 red peppers, de-seeded and quartered

4 Roma tomatoes, halved

6 garlic cloves, unpeeled

6 tbsp olive oil

salt and freshly ground black pepper

14oz (400g) dried red lentil rotini

2 tbsp finely chopped basil leaves

grated Parmesan cheese, to serve

serves 4 // time **50 mins** // **gluten free**

METHOD

1 Preheat the oven to 400°F (200°C). Line a baking sheet with parchment paper or aluminum foil. Place red peppers, tomatoes, and garlic cloves on the baking sheet and drizzle with 4 tbsp olive oil. Toss to coat, season well with salt and pepper, and spread out evenly on the baking sheet.

2 Roast on the top rack of the oven for 30 minutes, or until peppers start to blister and tomatoes collapse. Remove from the oven, place in a small, heatproof bowl and cover tightly with plastic wrap. Set aside to cool for at least 15 minutes.

3 When vegetables are cool enough to handle, peel and discard the skins from peppers, tomatoes, and garlic. Put vegetables in a blender or food processor. Add remaining 2 tbsp olive oil and pulse briefly until vegetables are broken down into a roughly textured sauce. Season with salt and pepper to taste. Place in a small saucepan.

4 Cook pasta according to the package instructions. When it is nearly cooked, gently heat red pepper and tomato sauce. Drain pasta and return it to the pot. Add sauce and basil and stir well to combine. Transfer to a serving dish, sprinkle with Parmesan, and serve immediately.

PASTA SWAP // dried chickpea rotini // dried black bean rotini // dried green lentil shells

SPAGHETTI WITH PANCETTA & POACHED EGG

The egg yolk creates a silky sauce for this rich and delicious dish. Mild millet spaghetti is tossed with crisped pancetta and Parmesan and topped with charred Brussels sprouts.

INGREDIENTS

1lb (450g) Brussels sprouts, trimmed and separated into individual leaves

3 tbsp olive oil

salt and freshly ground black pepper

4oz (115g) diced pancetta

1 garlic clove, crushed

14oz (400g) dried millet spaghetti

4 eggs

2 tbsp unsalted butter

1oz (30g) grated Parmesan cheese, plus extra to serve

serves 4 // time 50 mins // gluten free

METHOD

1 Preheat the oven to 450°F (230°C). Toss Brussels sprouts with 1 tbsp olive oil and season well with salt and pepper. Spread the leaves on a baking sheet and bake for 3 to 4 minutes until crisp at the edges. Watch carefully because they can burn quickly.

2 Heat remaining 2 tbsp olive oil in a large frying pan over medium heat. Cook pancetta for 2 to 3 minutes until starting to crisp. Add garlic and cook for 1 minute more before turning off the heat.

3 Begin heating water to poach eggs by filling a wide, deep skillet halfway with water and bringing to a boil. In a separate pot, cook pasta according to the package instructions. Drain, reserving 1 cup cooking water, and return spaghetti to the pot.

4 While pasta and pancetta cook, reduce the heat on the water for the eggs so the water is barely simmering. Crack eggs into individual bowls and gently slip them into the water one at a time. Poach eggs for 3 minutes until whites are opaque but yolks are still runny.

5 While eggs are cooking, quickly add reserved cooking water to the still-hot frying pan. Stir well to remove the browned bits of pancetta and garlic from the bottom of the pan. Add it to the pot with the cooked pasta, along with Brussels sprouts, butter, and Parmesan, and toss to combine.

6 Divide pasta evenly among 4 shallow bowls and top each bowl with a poached egg. Sprinkle with Parmesan and a bit of freshly ground black pepper. Serve immediately.

PASTA SWAP // spinach & millet flour spaghetti (see p30) // dried quinoa spaghetti

PEANUT & CHICKEN SWEET POTATO STIR-FRY

Sweet potato spirals are coated in a spicy peanut sauce and topped with marinated chicken in this easy and filling meal. Broiling the chicken adds flavor and a slightly charred exterior.

INGREDIENTS

2 small boneless, skinless chicken breasts

2 tbsp sunflower oil

2oz (60g) bean sprouts

8oz (225g) spiralized sweet potatoes (prepared weight)

2 scallions, very finely sliced on the diagonal

1 tbsp finely chopped cilantro, plus a few leaves to garnish

for the marinade

1 tbsp soy sauce

1 tbsp Chinese rice wine

1 tsp sesame oil

1 tsp chili oil

½ tsp sugar

1 garlic clove, crushed

1-in (2.5cm) piece fresh ginger root, peeled and grated

for the peanut sauce

2oz (60g) smooth peanut butter

1 tsp sesame oil

1 tsp chili oil

1 tbsp soy sauce

2 garlic cloves, finely chopped

2-in (5cm) piece fresh ginger root, finely chopped

serves 2 // time 30 mins, plus 1 hr to marinate // dairy free

METHOD

1 To make the marinade: in a small bowl, whisk together all ingredients until sugar has dissolved.

2 Place chicken on a cutting board, and cover with parchment paper. With a rolling pin or meat mallet, pound breasts to flatten them to even thicknesses. Place in a shallow dish and add marinade. Using your hands, rub marinade into chicken. Refrigerate, covered, for 1 to 3 hours, turning chicken occasionally in the dish.

3 To make the peanut sauce: put all ingredients, along with ½ cup water, in a blender. Blend until smooth.

4 Preheat the broiler to high and line a rimmed baking sheet with aluminum foil. Broil chicken for 3 to 4 minutes on each side until browned in spots and cooked through. Wrap loosely in foil and set aside.

5 In a large, non-stick frying pan, heat sunflower oil over medium heat. Add bean sprouts and cook for 1 minute. Add sweet potato noodles and cook, turning occasionally, until they soften but do not break, about 3 minutes. Add peanut sauce and continue to cook, stirring constantly, for another 2 to 3 minutes until sweet potatoes are soft and cooked through. Add scallions and cilantro, and toss gently to combine.

6 Portion noodles evenly among 2 serving bowls. Slice chicken and add equal amounts to each bowl. Garnish with cilantro and serve immediately.

CHILI VERDE BRAISED CHICKEN WITH BLACK BEAN PASTA

This light, delicate green chili is a world away from the usual heavy tomato and beef-based chilis. If tomatillos are unavailable, use green tomatoes. If you like it spicy, don't de-seed the jalapeño.

INGREDIENTS

1 lb (450g) tomatillos, de-husked and washed

½ sweet white onion, quartered

3 garlic cloves, unpeeled

1 jalapeño

1 tbsp olive oil

salt and freshly ground black pepper

juice of ½ lime

1¼ cups good quality chicken stock

½ tsp cumin

½ tsp coriander

large handful of cilantro

1½ lb (675g) skinless, boneless chicken thighs

10oz (300g) dried black bean penne

to serve

1 avocado, sliced

scallions, finely sliced

sour cream

serves 4 // time 2 hrs 30 mins // gluten free

METHOD

1 Preheat the oven to 450°F (230°C). Line a rimmed baking sheet with aluminum foil. Place whole tomatillos, onion, garlic, and jalapeño on the baking sheet, and rub with olive oil. Season well and roast on the top rack of the oven for 15 minutes, turning half way through, until soft and browning in places.

2 Remove vegetables from the oven and reduce heat to 300°F (150°C). Once they are cool enough to handle, de-seed jalapeño and peel garlic cloves. Place vegetables in a food processor, along with lime juice, chicken stock, cumin, coriander, and half of cilantro. Season with salt and pepper. Process until broken down to a rough liquid.

3 Arrange chicken in a single layer in the bottom of a Dutch oven. Pour tomatillo mixture over chicken and cook, covered, on the middle rack of the oven for 1 hour.

4 Remove the lid and cook for another 20 to 30 minutes until sauce thickens and reduces and chicken is very tender. Remove from the oven and use two forks to shred chicken.

5 Cook pasta according to the package instructions until just al dente. (Be careful not to overcook the pasta; it can quickly become mushy.) Drain and portion among 4 serving bowls. Add an equal portion of braised chicken to each bowl. Serve immediately, topped with avocado, scallions, remaining cilantro, and sour cream on the side.

PASTA SWAP // dried red lentil rotini // dried chickpea penne

SPAGHETTI WITH TOASTED HAZELNUTS & SAGE

In this simple dish, a buttery, aromatic breadcrumb mixture prepared with chopped hazelnuts and fresh sage enhances the dark, nutty flavor of spelt pasta. Sharp Pecorino adds a salty note.

INGREDIENTS

salt and freshly ground black pepper
14oz (400g) dried spelt spaghetti
2oz (60g) raw hazelnuts, roughly chopped
4 tbsp olive oil
4 tbsp butter
4oz (115g) breadcrumbs
2 tbsp very finely chopped sage
1oz (30g) grated Pecorino cheese, plus extra to serve

serves 4 // time 25 mins

METHOD

1 Cook pasta in boiling, salted water according to the package instructions.

2 Meanwhile, in a non-stick frying pan, dry-fry hazelnuts over medium heat, stirring frequently, until lightly golden brown. Remove from heat. Once cool, rub them well in a clean dish towel to remove skins. Finely chop and set aside. Wipe out the pan with paper towel.

3 In the same pan, heat 2 tbsp olive oil and 2 tbsp butter over medium heat. When butter starts to foam, add breadcrumbs and toss until well coated. Cook over medium-low heat for 2 minutes, stirring frequently, until breadcrumbs begin to color. Add sage and cook until breadcrumbs are deep golden brown. Remove from heat and stir in hazelnuts.

4 When spaghetti is al dente, drain well and return to the cooking pot. Add remaining 2 tbsp olive oil and 2 tbsp butter, season well with salt and pepper, and stir to combine. Add Pecorino and most of breadcrumb mixture, reserving some to garnish. Serve immediately, topped with extra Pecorino and reserved breadcrumbs.

PASTA SWAP // spelt & chestnut flour spaghetti (see p42) // dried einkorn spaghetti

PASTA E FAGIOLI WITH ROSEMARY & THYME

This is a traditional Italian peasant dish, made here with robust borlotti beans and gluten-free quinoa shells. For a tasty meat version, fry diced pancetta with the onions and vegetables.

INGREDIENTS

4oz (115g) dried borlotti beans, soaked overnight

2 tbsp olive oil, plus extra to toss

1 medium yellow onion, finely diced

1 large celery stalk, de-ribbed and finely diced

1 large carrot, finely diced

2 garlic cloves, minced

¼ cup dry white wine

14oz (400g) crushed tomatoes

2 cups vegetable stock

1 sprig of rosemary

1 large sprig of thyme

salt and freshly ground black pepper

4oz (115g) dried quinoa shells

2 tbsp finely chopped flat-leaf parsley

grated Parmesan cheese, to serve

serves 4 // time 1 hr 35 mins, plus overnight to soak // gluten free

METHOD

1 Drain beans and place in a heavy-bottomed saucepan. Cover with cold water and bring to a boil. Reduce to a simmer and cook, uncovered, for 30 minutes, or until beans are just cooked and still slightly firm. Drain and set aside.

2 In another large, heavy-bottomed saucepan, heat olive oil over medium heat. Add onion, celery, and carrot, and cook for 5 minutes until soft. Stir in garlic and cook for 1 minute more.

3 Increase heat to medium-high, add white wine, and let it simmer briefly. Add crushed tomatoes and vegetable stock and stir well to combine. Add rosemary and thyme sprigs and season well. Add partially cooked beans to the pan and bring to a boil. Reduce to a simmer and cook, covered, for 50 minutes, or until beans are very tender.

4 Meanwhile, cook pasta in boiling salted water according to the package instructions until just al dente. Drain and rinse under cold water. Drain again, then toss with a drizzle of olive oil to prevent sticking. Set aside to cool.

5 When beans are soft, add pasta and heat through, then remove from heat. Remove and discard thyme and rosemary sprigs. Stir in parsley, then taste and adjust seasoning. Transfer to a serving dish and serve immediately with plenty of Parmesan on top.

SINGAPORE SWEET POTATO NOODLES

This classic stir-fry recipe is best prepared in two-person portions to avoid overloading the wok. Take care to slice the vegetables finely for even cooking and beautiful presentation.

INGREDIENTS

4oz (115g) dried sweet potato vermicelli

2 tsp sesame oil, plus extra to toss

2 tbsp sunflower oil

8oz (225g) raw peeled and de-veined shrimp

salt and freshly ground black pepper

¼ large red onion, very finely sliced

1 carrot, julienned

¼ large red pepper, julienned

1 garlic clove, very finely chopped

1-in (2.5cm) piece fresh ginger root, very finely chopped

½ tsp curry powder

¼ tsp turmeric

2 tsp sugar

2½oz (75g) white cabbage, cored and finely shredded

2oz (60g) bean sprouts

1 tbsp Chinese rice wine

1 tbsp soy sauce

2 scallions, finely sliced on the diagonal, to garnish

serves 2 // time 25 mins // dairy free

METHOD

1 In a medium, heatproof bowl, cover noodles with boiling water. Soak for 15 minutes, or until soft. Then drain and rinse under cold water to cool. Toss with a drizzle of sesame oil to prevent sticking.

2 In a wok, heat 1 tsp sesame oil and 1 tbsp sunflower oil over medium heat. Season shrimp with salt and pepper. Add to the wok and stir-fry for 2 minutes until they turn pink. Remove from the wok and set aside.

3 Heat remaining 1 tsp sesame oil and remaining 1 tbsp sunflower oil. Add onion, carrot, and red pepper. Cook, stirring constantly, for 1 minute. Add garlic, ginger, curry powder, turmeric, and sugar. Cook for another 1 to 2 minutes until spices are fragrant. Add cabbage and bean sprouts and cook for 1 to 2 minutes until starting to wilt. Toss well and add noodles.

4 Continue to stir constantly until noodles are coated in spices. Season with a little salt, and stir in Chinese rice wine and soy sauce. Return shrimp to the pan and toss to combine. Serve immediately, garnished with sliced scallions.

NOODLE SWAP // dried rice vermicelli // dried glass noodles // shirataki noodles

SCALLOPS WITH SORGHUM & SQUID INK TAGLIATELLE

This beautiful black pasta looks stunning when paired with the bright red tomatoes, white scallops, and green arugula. Serve this rich dish as an appetizer or light lunch.

INGREDIENTS

2 tbsp olive oil

2 tbsp unsalted butter

8oz (225g) cherry tomatoes, halved

salt and freshly ground black pepper

1 batch of sorghum & squid ink dough (see p32), cut into tagliatelle (see p44)

8oz (225g) bay scallops

2 garlic cloves, crushed

2oz (60g) baby arugula

serves 4 // time 40 mins // gluten free

METHOD

1 In a large frying pan or cast-iron skillet, heat olive oil and butter over medium heat. Once bubbling, add tomatoes, cut-side down, and cook for 2 minutes without turning.

2 Meanwhile, bring a pot of salted water to a boil. Cook pasta until al dente, about 3 minutes. Drain pasta, reserving 2 cups cooking water.

3 Flip tomatoes, add scallops, and cook over high heat for 2 to 3 minutes. Add garlic and cook for 1 minute more. Add reserved cooking water and season well with salt and pepper.

4 When the liquid begins to bubble, add cooked pasta and arugula. Gently toss. Taste and season with salt and pepper if needed. Serve immediately.

PASTA SWAP // almond & tapioca flour tagliatelle (see p40) // dried gluten-free squid ink pasta

RICE PENNE WITH ROASTED BUTTERNUT SAUCE

Mild brown rice penne is tossed with a wonderfully creamy sauce that gets its sweetness from roasted butternut squash. Chilies, smoked paprika, and fried sage add spiciness and depth of flavor.

INGREDIENTS

7oz (200g) butternut squash, peeled and cubed (prepared weight)

2 tbsp olive oil

salt and freshly ground black pepper

2 garlic cloves, crushed

1 mild red chile pepper, de-seeded and finely chopped

2 tbsp very finely chopped sage leaves

¼ tsp smoked paprika

5fl oz (150ml) whipping cream

1oz (30g) grated Parmesan cheese, plus extra to serve

12oz (350g) dried brown rice penne

serves 4 // time 1 hr // gluten free

METHOD

1 Preheat the oven to 400°F (200°C). Line a baking sheet with parchment paper. In a medium bowl, toss butternut squash with 1 tbsp olive oil and season well with salt and pepper. Spread on the baking sheet and roast for 25 to 30 minutes, turning occasionally, until cooked through and golden brown. Remove from the oven and set aside to cool.

2 In a non-stick frying pan, heat remaining 1 tbsp olive oil over medium-low heat. Add garlic, chilies, and sage, and cook for 1 to 2 minutes, until fragrant and beginning to color. Remove from heat and stir in smoked paprika.

3 Place cooled butternut squash, fried aromatics, whipping cream, and Parmesan into a blender and blend until smooth. Transfer sauce to a small saucepan.

4 Cook pasta according to the package instructions. When it is nearly cooked, gently heat sauce. Drain pasta well and return it to the cooking pot. Add heated sauce and stir well to combine. Transfer to a serving dish, top with extra Parmesan, and serve immediately.

MUNG BEAN NOODLES WITH BASIL-FRIED SQUID

Also called glass noodles, mung bean noodles have a robust and chewy texture that perfectly complements tender squid. The distinct anise-like flavor of Thai basil really makes this dish stand out.

INGREDIENTS

6oz (175g) dried wide mung bean noodles

1 tbsp sunflower oil

½ small red onion, sliced

2 garlic cloves, thinly sliced

½ red pepper, de-seeded and finely chopped, or more to taste

8oz (225g) squid bodies, cleaned and tentacles removed, thinly sliced

handful of whole Thai basil leaves

for the sauce

1 tsp sugar

1 tbsp fish sauce

1 tbsp oyster sauce

2 tbsp soy sauce

serves 2 // time 1 hr // dairy free

METHOD

1 Place noodles in a large, heatproof bowl and cover with boiling water. Soak for 30 minutes, then set aside to drain well.

2 To make the sauce: in a small bowl, whisk together all ingredients and set aside.

3 In a large wok, heat sunflower oil over high heat. Add onion and cook for 2 minutes, then add garlic and red pepper and cook for 1 minute more until fragrant. Add squid and cook for another 2 minutes, or until it becomes opaque.

4 Add sauce to the pan and let simmer briefly. Add noodles and cook for 3 to 4 minutes until well softened. Remove from heat and stir in Thai basil so that it wilts. Transfer to a serving dish and serve immediately.

NOODLE SWAP // dried rice vermicelli // dried rice stick noodles

SPICY TOMATO & SHRIMP PASTA

This simple but deeply flavored sauce pairs well with lighter, mildly flavored pastas. Use shapes such as fettuccine, spaghetti, or angel hair to complement the textures of the dish.

INGREDIENTS

1lb (450g) large shell-on raw shrimp (preferably with heads)

2 tbsp olive oil, plus extra to toss

1 small yellow onion, very finely diced

2 garlic cloves, crushed

½ tsp red pepper flakes

28oz (794g) can crushed tomatoes

salt and freshly ground black pepper

1 batch of almond & tapioca flour dough (see p40), cut into long ribbons (see p46)

2 tbsp finely chopped flat-leaf parsley

serves 4 // time 45 mins // dairy free // gluten free

METHOD

1 Peel and de-head shrimp, reserving shells and heads. Slice shrimp horizontally in half, de-vein, and set aside in the refrigerator until needed.

2 To make the shrimp stock: place shrimp heads and shells in a medium, heavy-bottomed saucepan and cover with 2 cups cold water. Bring to a boil, then reduce to a simmer, and cook, uncovered, for 10 to 15 minutes until liquid reduces by half. Strain out shells and heads, and set stock aside to cool.

3 In a medium, heavy-bottomed saucepan, heat olive oil over medium heat. Add onion and cook for 3 to 5 minutes until soft but not brown. Add garlic and red pepper flakes, reduce heat to low, and cook for 1 minute more.

4 Add tomatoes and shrimp stock, and bring to a boil. Reduce to a simmer and cook, uncovered, for 20 to 30 minutes until sauce thickens and reduces. Season well with salt and pepper.

5 While sauce simmers, cook pasta in boiling, salted water until al dente, about 4 minutes. Drain and toss with a drizzle of olive oil to prevent sticking.

6 Add raw shrimp and parsley to sauce, reserving some parsley for garnish. Cook over medium heat for 1 to 2 minutes until shrimp turns opaque and curls up.

7 Toss pasta with sauce and serve immediately, topped with reserved parsley and a drizzle of olive oil.

PASTA SWAP // dried brown rice spaghetti // dried quinoa angel hair

SHAVED ASPARAGUS, MINT & EDAMAME SPAGHETTI

This vibrant green sauce is perfect for a light meal. Mint provides an unexpected and refreshing flavor that is delicious served with the tender asparagus and edamame.

INGREDIENTS

salt and freshly ground black pepper

8oz (225g) large asparagus, trimmed

4oz (115g) frozen shelled edamame

14oz (400g) dried edamame spaghetti

2 tbsp olive oil, plus extra to serve

1 large leek, white parts only, trimmed and julienned

1 large garlic clove, crushed

4oz (115g) ricotta cheese

1 large handful of fresh mint leaves, finely chopped, plus extra whole leaves to garnish

2 tbsp grated Parmesan cheese, plus extra to serve

serves 4 // time 30 mins // gluten free

METHOD

1 Bring a large pot of salted water to a boil. To prepare asparagus, place each spear flat on a chopping board and use a peeler to shave into very thin slices.

2 Cook edamame in the boiling water for 1 minute. Remove with a slotted spoon and put into a bowl of iced water.

3 Add pasta to the boiling water and cook according to the package instructions until just al dente. When pasta is cooked, drain and reserve ½ cup cooking water. Set pasta aside.

4 Meanwhile, when spaghetti is nearly cooked, heat olive oil in a large, non-stick frying pan. Add asparagus and leek and cook for 2 minutes, stirring frequently, until asparagus starts to soften. Add garlic and edamame and cook for 1 minute more. Remove from heat.

5 Add ricotta and ¼ cup reserved cooking water to the pasta pot. Whisk until smooth, adding more cooking water as necessary. Add asparagus mixture to the pot and mix together over low heat.

6 Add spaghetti back to the pot, along with chopped mint and Parmesan. Toss well. Season well with salt and pepper. Portion onto 4 serving plates and serve immediately with more Parmesan, mint leaves, and a drizzle of olive oil on top.

PASTA SWAP // dried green lentil spaghetti // spelt & chestnut flour spaghetti (see p42)

BLACK SESAME & COCONUT CURRY BOWL

By themselves, shirataki noodles have very little taste, so pan-frying them in the curry sauce allows them to absorb all the gently spiced flavors of this simple vegan dish.

INGREDIENTS

3 tbsp coconut oil

½ red onion, finely chopped

2 garlic cloves, finely chopped

1-in (2.5cm) piece fresh ginger root, finely chopped

½ large red pepper, diced

5½oz (150g) mushrooms, peeled and quartered

2 tsp curry powder

¼ tsp chili powder (optional)

14fl oz (400ml) can coconut milk

4fl oz (120ml) good quality vegetable stock

10oz (300g) sweet potato, peeled and diced into ½-in (1cm) cubes

2 x 7oz (200g) packages shirataki noodles

to serve

handful of fresh cilantro leaves

2 scallions, trimmed and sliced on the diagonal

½ tsp black sesame seeds

serves 4 // time 40 mins // gluten free // vegan

METHOD

1 In a medium, heavy-bottomed saucepan, melt 2 tbsp coconut oil over medium heat. Add onion and cook for 2 to 3 minutes until soft but not brown. Incorporate garlic and ginger and cook for 1 minute more.

2 Add red pepper and mushrooms and cook for 2 to 3 minutes until they start to deepen in color. Add remaining 1 tbsp coconut oil, curry powder, and chili powder (if using), and stir well to combine. Reduce heat to low and cook for 1 minute until spices release fragrance.

3 Incorporate coconut milk and vegetable stock. Add sweet potatoes and bring to a boil. Reduce to a simmer and cook, uncovered, for 10 to 12 minutes until sweet potatoes are soft.

4 Meanwhile, bring a pot of water to a boil. Transfer shirataki noodles to a colander and rinse thoroughly under cold running water for at least 30 seconds to rinse off packaging liquid. In the pot of boiling water, cook noodles for 2 minutes. Drain well, and set aside to cool completely.

5 Heat a large, non-stick frying pan over high heat. Once cool, dry-fry noodles for 2 minutes, stirring constantly. Add most of sauce to noodles and cook for another 2 minutes until the sauce is mostly absorbed.

6 Portion noodles into 4 serving bowls and top with equal amounts curried vegetables and remaining sauce. Garnish with equal amounts cilantro, scallions, and sesame seeds, and serve immediately.

SPAGHETTI SQUASH WITH PANCETTA & PARMESAN

With its noodle-like strands, spaghetti squash mimics the texture of pasta, but it can be a little bland on its own. Frying it with pancetta and garlic results in a hearty, flavorful dish.

INGREDIENTS

1 small spaghetti squash, about 1½lb (675g), halved and de-seeded

2 tbsp olive oil

4oz (115g) pancetta, diced

1 garlic clove, crushed

½ tsp red pepper flakes

2 tbsp unsalted butter

salt and freshly ground black pepper

grated Parmesan cheese, to serve

serves 4 // time 1 hr 5 mins // gluten free

METHOD

1 Preheat the oven to 375°F (190°C) and line a rimmed baking sheet with parchment paper. Place squash halves cut-side down on the baking sheet and add 2 tbsp water to the sheet. Roast for 30 to 40 minutes until the flesh is soft. Set aside to cool.

2 When squash has cooled, use a large metal spoon to scoop out the flesh and separate it into strands. In a large, non-stick frying pan, heat olive oil over medium heat. Add pancetta and cook for 3 to 4 minutes until brown and crispy. Reduce heat to low, add garlic and red pepper flakes, and cook for 1 minute more.

3 Add butter and let it melt, then add squash and toss to combine. Taste and season with salt and pepper. Increase heat to high and cook for 3 to 4 minutes, turning frequently, until golden brown in places. Transfer to a serving dish, top with Parmesan, and serve immediately.

CORN FARFALLE WITH SWEET CORN & BACON

Tangy goat cheese and salty bacon complement the sweetness of the corn in this creamy sauce, which is served over homemade corn pasta. Use fresh corn for the best flavor.

INGREDIENTS

salt and freshly ground black pepper

2 tbsp olive oil

1 small red onion, finely chopped

6 slices bacon, diced

2 garlic cloves, crushed

2 tbsp unsalted butter

2 ears corn, kernels cut from cobs, about 7oz (200g) kernels in total

1 cup good quality chicken stock

½ cup heavy cream

3oz (85g) soft goat cheese

1 batch of corn flour dough (see p38), shaped into farfalle (see p52)

1 tbsp finely chopped basil, plus extra to serve

grated Parmesan cheese, to serve

serves 4 // time 45 mins // gluten free

METHOD

1 Bring a pot of salted water to a boil. In a large frying pan or cast-iron skillet, heat olive oil over medium heat. When hot, add onion and cook for 3 to 4 minutes until soft but not brown. Add bacon and cook for another 3 to 4 minutes until bacon starts to crisp. Stir in garlic and cook for 1 minute more.

2 Use a slotted spoon to remove onion and bacon from the pan, leaving behind most of the oil. Melt butter in the pan, add corn kernels, and cook over medium heat for 1 to 2 minutes until they darken in color. Add chicken stock and cook for 1 to 2 minutes more until kernels are tender.

3 Remove from heat and season well. Transfer corn mixture to a blender and add heavy cream and goat cheese. Blend until completely smooth.

4 Cook pasta in the boiling water for 3 to 4 minutes until just al dente.

5 Meanwhile, transfer corn sauce and bacon mixture to a small saucepan and heat gently until just warmed through. Remove from heat and stir in basil.

6 Drain pasta and return it to the cooking pot. Add sauce to pasta and stir well to combine. Serve immediately with extra basil and Parmesan scattered on top.

PASTA SWAP // dried brown rice farfalle // dried corn fusilli // dried einkorn fusilli

PAPPARDELLE & SLOW-COOKED BEEF RIB RAGU

The oven does most of the work to make this rich and savory classic Italian braise. Serve it with freshly made pappardelle or fettuccine to soak up the robust flavors of the sauce.

INGREDIENTS

2 tbsp olive oil

salt and freshly ground black pepper

1½lb (675g) bone-in short ribs

1 onion, peeled and finely chopped

2 carrots, peeled and finely chopped

2 celery stalks, trimmed, peeled, and finely chopped

2 slices thick-cut bacon, finely diced

2 garlic cloves, crushed

1 tbsp unsalted butter

1 tbsp all-purpose flour (white rice or potato flour for gluten free)

1 tbsp tomato paste

8fl oz (240ml) robust red wine, such as merlot

16fl oz (500ml) good quality beef stock

½ tsp sugar

4 sprigs of thyme, plus extra to garnish

1 batch of almond & tapioca flour dough (see p40), cut into pappardelle (see p44)

grated Parmesan cheese, to serve (optional)

serves 4–6 // time 3 hrs // gluten free

METHOD

1 Pre-heat the oven to 350°F (180°C). In a 5-quart (4.75l) Dutch oven, heat 1 tbsp olive oil over medium heat. Liberally season both sides of ribs with salt and pepper. Brown them for 3 to 4 minutes on each side until a dark crust forms. Remove from the pot and set aside.

2 Add remaining 1 tbsp olive oil, onion, carrots, and celery to the pot. Cook over medium-low heat, stirring occasionally for 3 to 5 minutes until they start to soften but not brown. Raise heat to medium-high and add bacon. Cook for 2 minutes, or until it starts to crisp. Finally, stir in garlic and cook for 1 minute more without letting garlic burn.

3 Reduce heat to low, add butter to the pot, and let it melt. Add flour and tomato paste, stir well to combine, and cook for another 1 to 2 minutes, stirring constantly.

4 Gradually add wine, stirring constantly to release browned bits from the bottom of the pot. Stir in beef stock, sugar, and thyme. Return ribs to the pot. Cover and transfer to the oven. Cook for 2 hours.

5 Remove from the oven and remove the lid. Turn ribs over in sauce and return to the oven. Cook, uncovered, for another 30 minutes, or until sauce reduces. Remove from the oven and let cool.

6 When cool enough to handle, remove ribs from the pot. Shred all meat from the bones. Remove thyme stems from sauce. Return meat to the pot and stir.

7 Bring a pot of salted water to a boil. Cook pasta for 5 to 6 minutes until just al dente. Drain. Gently reheat sauce if necessary. Serve rib sauce over pasta, topped with fresh thyme and Parmesan, if using.

PASTA SWAP // corn flour pappardelle (see p38) **//** dried rice fettuccine

BLACK BEAN PASTA WITH MUHAMMARA & WALNUTS

Deep, bitter, sweet, and sour, pomegranate molasses helps create the complex flavors of the muhammara, a spicy pepper paste suitable for vegans. For non-vegetarians, Pecorino cheese perfectly offsets the sauce's piquancy.

INGREDIENTS

8oz (225g) dried black bean spaghetti

chopped walnuts, to serve

shaved Pecorino cheese, to serve (optional)

for the muhammara

4oz (115g) walnuts, roughly chopped

12oz (340g) jar fire-roasted red peppers, drained and patted dry

1oz (30g) panko breadcrumbs

4 tbsp olive oil

1 large garlic clove, crushed

½ tsp cumin

¼ tsp cayenne

1 tsp lemon juice

2 tsp pomegranate molasses

salt and freshly ground black pepper

serves 4 // time 30 mins

METHOD

1 To make the muhammara: place all ingredients in a food processor, along with 2 tbsp cold water. Pulse until a nearly smooth paste forms, like the texture of pesto.

2 Cook pasta according to the package instructions. Drain, reserving ½ cup cooking water in the pot, and set pasta aside. Add muhammara to reserved cooking water and heat through.

3 Add pasta to the pan and toss well. Serve immediately with walnuts and Pecorino on top, if using.

PASTA SWAP // dried red lentil spaghetti // dried brown rice fettuccine // spelt & chestnut flour spaghetti (see p42)

BLECS WITH HAZELNUT BROWNED BUTTER & PECORINO

The nutty flavor of the buckwheat pasta is perfectly complemented by the aromatic browned butter, sharp greens, and salty cheese. This is a rich and filling dish.

INGREDIENTS

salt and freshly ground black pepper

2oz (60g) hazelnuts, roughly chopped

4oz (115g) unsalted butter

1 batch of buckwheat flour dough (see p36), cut into blecs (see p56)

6oz (175g) de-ribbed and roughly chopped mustard greens, washed

2oz (60g) shaved Pecorino cheese

serves 4–6 // time 20 mins // gluten free

METHOD

1 Bring a large pot of salted water to a boil. In a large sauté pan, dry-fry hazelnuts over medium-low heat for 3 to 4 minutes, stirring occasionally, until they start to brown. Remove from heat. Once cool, rub them well in a clean dish towel to remove skins. Roughly chop and set aside. Wipe out the pan.

2 Put butter in the pan, and melt over medium heat. Continue to cook for 2 to 3 minutes, letting it bubble and stirring constantly. Pour into a heatproof bowl as soon as it reaches a nutty brown color. Wipe out the pan again.

3 Cook pasta in the pot of boiling water for 3 to 4 minutes until just al dente. Drain, and reserve 1 cup cooking water.

4 Pour a bit of browned butter into the sauté pan to coat the bottom, and heat gently. Add mustard greens, season well with pepper and a little bit of salt (Pecorino is already salty), and cook over high heat until greens start to wilt. Add pasta, three-quarters of hazelnuts, and remaining browned butter. Toss well to combine, gradually adding 1oz (30g) Pecorino and reserved cooking water a tablespoon at a time, as needed, until sauce combines.

5 Continue to toss pasta until heated through and thoroughly coated. Transfer to serving dishes. Top with equal amounts remaining hazelnuts and remaining 1oz (30g) Pecorino. Season to taste with pepper and serve immediately.

PASTA SWAP // spelt & chestnut flour blecs (see p42)

ALMOND FETTUCCINE WITH CRAB & LEMON SAUCE

Homemade fettuccine is tossed in a light and tangy sauce inspired by avgolemono, the traditional Greek sauce made with lemon and egg. Succulent crab and fresh dill elevate the flavors of the dish.

INGREDIENTS

1½ cups good quality chicken stock

3 eggs

juice of 1 lemon, plus zest to garnish

1 tsp tapioca flour

salt and freshly ground black pepper

*8oz (225g) crab meat, separated
    with a fork*

*1 batch of almond & tapioca flour dough (see p40),
    cut into fettuccine (see p44)*

2 tbsp finely chopped dill

grated Parmesan cheese, to serve

serves 4 // **time 25 mins** // **gluten free**

METHOD

1 In a small, heavy-bottomed saucepan, heat chicken stock over medium heat until just beginning to boil. Meanwhile, in a medium, heatproof bowl, whisk together eggs, lemon juice, and tapioca flour until smooth.

2 When chicken stock is hot, pour it into egg mixture in a thin, steady stream, whisking constantly. Return mixture to the saucepan over medium heat, and continue whisking until mixture thickens, then remove from heat. Taste and season with salt and pepper. Stir in crab meat, let it warm up, then set aside.

3 Bring a pot of salted water to a boil, and cook pasta for 3 to 4 minutes until just al dente. Drain pasta well and return it to the cooking pot. Add sauce and dill and stir to combine. Transfer to a serving dish, garnish with lemon zest and Parmesan, and serve immediately.

PASTA SWAP // beet & rice flour fettuccine (see p42) // dried brown rice fettuccine

CAULIFLOWER & CASHEW CARBONARA

This vegan version of the classic pasta dish is made creamy with a silky cashew sauce, and nutritional yeast mimics the sharp saltiness of Parmesan cheese.

INGREDIENTS

2 tbsp olive oil

1 small white onion, finely chopped

2 garlic cloves, crushed

2oz (60g) raw cashews

2 cups vegetable stock

10oz (300g) cauliflower florets, chopped into small pieces

salt and freshly ground black pepper

14oz (400g) dried spelt spaghetti

nutritional yeast, to serve

serves **4** // time **40 mins** // **dairy free** // **vegan**

METHOD

1 In a medium, heavy-bottomed saucepan, heat olive oil over medium heat. Add onion and cook, stirring occasionally, for 5 minutes until soft but not brown. Add garlic and cook for 1 minute more.

2 Add cashews and vegetable stock to the pan. Reduce heat to low and cook, covered, for 5 minutes. Add cauliflower florets and raise heat to bring to a boil. Then reduce heat to low and continue to cook, covered, for 5 to 7 minutes until cauliflower is soft. Remove from heat, uncover, and set aside to cool.

3 When mixture is cool, transfer to a blender or food processor and blend until completely smooth. Taste and season well. Pour sauce into a small saucepan.

4 Cook pasta according to the package instructions. When it is nearly cooked, gently heat sauce. Drain pasta well and return it to the cooking pot. Add heated sauce and stir to combine. Serve immediately with nutritional yeast sprinkled on top.

PASTA SWAP // spelt & chestnut flour spaghetti (see p42) // dried brown rice spaghetti

SPAGHETTI WITH SMOKED SARDINES & RAISINS

This version of the Sicilian classic "pasta con le sarde" uses canned sardines rather than fresh grilled ones. It has a delicious sweet and sour flavor with many contrasting textures.

INGREDIENTS

1oz (30g) pine nuts

14oz (400g) dried spelt or chickpea spaghetti

2 tbsp olive oil

2oz (60g) unsalted butter

1 fennel bulb, trimmed, halved, and finely sliced, about 9oz (250g) prepared weight

8fl oz (240ml) white wine

salt and freshly ground black pepper

2oz (60g) golden raisins

4oz (115g) can smoked sardines, broken into large pieces, plus oil

grated Parmesan cheese, to serve (optional)

serves 4 // time 45 mins

METHOD

1 In a cast-iron pan, dry-fry pine nuts over medium heat, stirring frequently, until they start to brown in places. Remove from the pan and set aside to cool. Wipe out the pan.

2 Cook pasta according to the package instructions. Drain and reserve 1 cup cooking water.

3 While pasta is cooking, heat olive oil and 1oz (30g) butter in the cast-iron pan. When hot, add fennel and cook over medium-low heat for 10 minutes, stirring frequently, until soft and slightly browned.

4 Add white wine and reserved cooking water and cook over high heat until it bubbles and starts to reduce. Whisk in remaining 1oz (30g) butter. Season well with salt and pepper. Add raisins and sardines, along with packaging oil, to sauce. Cook for another 1 to 2 minutes, stirring occasionally but being careful not to break up sardines.

5 Return pasta to the pot and add sardine sauce. Toss well. Cook over high heat until pasta absorbs any excess liquid. Stir in pine nuts, reserving some for garnish. Transfer to serving dishes. Very lightly top with Parmesan (if using), reserved pine nuts, and black pepper. Serve immediately.

PASTA SWAP // dried quinoa spaghetti // chickpea flour spaghetti (see p34)

MISO JAPANESE EGGPLANT & BUCKWHEAT NOODLES

Japanese eggplants are long, thin, and have very few seeds, but you can also use any young eggplants you can find. With its umami flavor, this dish tastes light while being filling.

INGREDIENTS

2 firm Japanese eggplants, trimmed and halved lengthwise, then in half widthwise

salt

8oz (225g) dried 100% buckwheat noodles

sesame oil, to toss

1 tbsp sesame seeds

1 tbsp sunflower oil, plus extra for greasing

6oz (175g) very finely sliced green cabbage

6oz (175g) bean sprouts

1 tbsp soy sauce

4 large scallions, trimmed and very finely sliced on the diagonal

2 tbsp chopped cilantro leaves, plus whole leaves to garnish

for the glaze

2 tbsp white miso paste

4 tbsp mirin

1½ tbsp sugar

2 tsp sesame oil

serves 4 // time 50 mins // dairy free

METHOD

1 Preheat the oven to 425°F (220°C). Lightly score the cut-side of eggplants with the tip of a sharp knife to make a criss-cross design. Place cut-side down on a lightly oiled baking sheet and transfer to the top rack of the oven. Bake for 10 to 15 minutes until soft.

2 Meanwhile, bring a large pot of salted water to a boil. To make the glaze: in a small saucepan, whisk together miso paste and 4 tbsp hot water. Then whisk in mirin, sugar, and sesame oil. Bring briefly to a boil, whisking constantly until sugar has dissolved. Remove from heat and set aside.

3 Cook noodles in the boiling water according to the package instructions until just al dente, then drain and rinse briefly under cold water. Toss with a drizzle of sesame oil to prevent sticking.

4 When eggplant is soft, remove from the oven and turn the oven on to a high broil. Line the baking sheet with foil and arrange eggplants cut-side up on the sheet. Brush cut-sides with glaze. Return to the top rack of the oven and broil until well browned and crisp on top, about 10 minutes. Pull eggplants out of the oven occasionally to brush with more glaze when it has been absorbed (about 3 times). Sprinkle with sesame seeds and broil for one last time until sesame seeds are brown.

5 Heat sunflower oil in a wok over medium heat. Add cabbage and bean sprouts and stir-fry for 1 minute. Stir soy sauce into remaining glaze. Add noodles, scallions, and glaze to the wok and cook for 1 minute more until heated through. Add chopped cilantro and toss well to combine. Portion onto 4 serving dishes, and top each with 2 pieces of eggplant. Garnish with cilantro leaves and serve immediately.

NOODLE SWAP // dried einkorn spaghetti // buckwheat flour spaghetti (see p36)

FIERY DAN DAN NOODLES WITH PORK

This spicy, saucy dish gets its heat from Sichuan peppercorns and red pepper flakes. For a gluten-free version, replace the soy sauce with liquid aminos.

INGREDIENTS

1 tsp dried Sichuan peppercorns

8oz (225g) dried millet noodles

2 tbsp sunflower oil, plus extra to toss

8oz (225g) ground pork

2 garlic cloves, crushed

1-in (2.5cm) piece fresh ginger root, finely grated

½ tsp red pepper flakes

½ tsp sugar

2½ tbsp soy sauce

½ small red onion, finely sliced

½ red pepper, de-seeded and finely julienned

1 carrot, finely julienned

1 tbsp rice wine vinegar

1 tbsp Chinese rice wine

2 scallions, trimmed and very finely sliced on the diagonal, to garnish

2 tbsp roughly chopped salted peanuts, to garnish

serves 2 // time 25 mins // dairy free

METHOD

1 In a small, non-stick frying pan, dry-fry Sichuan peppercorns over low heat for 2 minutes, or until they darken and become fragrant. Remove from the pan and set aside to cool, then grind to a powder with a mortar and pestle.

2 Cook noodles according to the package instructions until just al dente. Drain, then rinse under cold water. Drain again, then toss with a drizzle of sunflower oil to prevent sticking. Set aside to cool.

3 In a wok, heat 1 tbsp sunflower oil over high heat. Add ground pork and stir constantly for 5 minutes, or until it is no longer pink. Then reduce heat to medium and continue to cook for 2 to 3 minutes until it darkens and begins to release oil. Add Sichuan peppercorns, garlic, ginger, red pepper flakes, sugar, and ½ tbsp soy sauce. Reduce heat to low and cook for 1 minute until the moisture has evaporated.

4 Transfer mixture to a bowl. Heat remaining 1 tbsp sunflower oil in the wok, add onion, pepper, and carrot, and stir-fry for 2 minutes until just cooked. Add noodles and pork to the wok, along with vinegar, rice wine, and remaining 2 tbsp soy sauce. Stir-fry for 2 minutes until heated through. Portion among 2 serving bowls, garnish with scallions and peanuts, and serve immediately.

NOODLE SWAP // buckwheat flour noodles (see p36) // dried buckwheat soba noodles

SPELT PASTA WITH GRIDDLED RADICCHIO & PROSCIUTTO

Simple but full of flavor, this dish calls for grilling wedges of vibrant purple and white radicchio, which mellows their bitterness and makes for a beautiful presentation.

INGREDIENTS

8 slices prosciutto

1 head radicchio, about 10oz (300g)

4 tbsp olive oil

salt and freshly ground black pepper

1 batch of spelt & chestnut flour dough (see p42), cut into long ribbons (see p46)

2 tbsp butter

2 garlic cloves, crushed

4 tbsp grated Parmesan cheese

serves 4 // time **30 mins**

METHOD

1 Preheat the oven to 350°F (180°C). On a baking sheet, spread prosciutto in a single layer. Cook on the top rack of the oven for 5 minutes, or until crisp and browned, then remove from the oven and let cool on the tray. Break it up into thin pieces.

2 Cut radicchio in half, then cut each half into thin wedges, taking care to keep the bottom of each wedge held together with a piece of the root. Toss radicchio with 2 tbsp olive oil and season well.

3 Heat a cast-iron grill pan over high heat. When hot, add radicchio wedges and cook for 3 to 4 minutes, turning occasionally until they are scorched at the edges. (This may need to be done in several batches.) As radicchio is ready, place it on a plate to cool.

4 Bring a pot of salted water to a boil, and cook pasta for 3 to 4 minutes until just al dente. Drain, reserving 1 cup of cooking water.

5 In the pasta pot, heat remaining 2 tbsp olive oil and butter over medium heat. Add garlic and cook for 1 minute, or until golden brown. Add reserved cooking water and allow it to boil, then add pasta. Season well and toss to combine. Add radicchio, most of prosciutto, and most of Parmesan. Toss again. Serve immediately with remaining prosciutto and Parmesan scattered over the top.

PASTA SWAP // dried spelt spaghetti // dried einkorn spaghetti

BEET TAGLIATELLE WITH GOAT CHEESE & FRIED SAGE

The use of simple, fresh ingredients with strong flavors and contrasting colors works very well with the deep pink of this homemade pasta.

INGREDIENTS

salt and freshly ground black pepper

2oz (60g) unsalted butter

1/2 cup olive oil, plus extra to garnish

2 garlic cloves, crushed

1 bunch fresh sage (2 tbsp finely chopped, and remaining left whole for optional garnish)

1 batch of beet & rice flour dough (see p28), cut into tagliatelle (see p46)

4oz (115g) soft goat cheese, roughly crumbled

serves **4** // time **25 mins** // **gluten free** // **vegetarian**

METHOD

1 Bring a large pot of salted water to a boil. In a medium frying pan, heat butter and ¼ cup olive oil over medium heat until butter melts. Add garlic and cook, stirring constantly, for 1 to 2 minutes until garlic starts to color but does not brown.

2 Add finely chopped sage and cook for 1 to 2 minutes until it begins to crisp. Remove from heat and season generously with salt and pepper. Set aside.

3 Meanwhile, to deep-fry whole sage as an optional garnish: in a small skillet, heat remaining ¼ cup olive oil over medium-high heat. Working in batches, carefully place 6 to 8 whole sage leaves in oil and deep fry until crisp but not brown and no longer sizzling. Remove with a fork and transfer to a plate lined with paper towel to drain. Season with salt.

4 Cook pasta in the boiling water. Drain, reserving 1 cup cooking water. Return pasta to the pot. Add garlic and chopped sage mixture, and toss well. Add most of goat cheese, and gently mix, adding cooking water a tablespoon at a time as necessary to bring sauce together.

5 Portion into 4 serving bowls. Garnish with reserved goat cheese, whole fried sage leaves (if using), pepper, and a drizzle of olive oil. Serve immediately before cheese entirely melts.

PASTA SWAP // spinach & millet flour tagliatelle (see p30) // dried quinoa spaghetti

ROASTED CAULIFLOWER & MINT ORECCHIETTE

The hearty yet delicately shaped chickpea pasta is a perfect partner for creamy roasted cauliflower and light, fresh herbs. If you can't find orange cauliflower, substitute with white cauliflower.

INGREDIENTS

salt and freshly ground black pepper
½ batch of chickpea flour dough (see p34), shaped into orecchiette (see p54)
2 tbsp unsalted butter
2 tbsp olive oil
2 tbsp finely chopped flat-leaf parsley
2 tbsp fresh mint
grated Parmesan cheese, to serve

for the cauliflower

4 tbsp olive oil
2 garlic cloves, crushed
1 tsp red pepper flakes
1 lb (450g) orange cauliflower florets

serves 4 // time 25 mins // gluten free

METHOD

1 Preheat the oven to 400°F (200°C). Bring a large pot of salted water to a boil. To make the cauliflower: in a large bowl, mix olive oil, garlic, and red pepper flakes. Season with salt and pepper to taste. Add cauliflower and toss with your hands, making sure seasoning is rubbed in well.

2 Evenly spread cauliflower in a large, metal roasting pan. Transfer to the top rack of the oven and roast for 15 minutes, or until just cooked and browned in places.

3 Cook orecchiette in the boiling water for 5 to 6 minutes until just al dente. Drain and reserve 1 cup cooking water.

4 In a large, cast-iron skillet, melt butter and olive oil over medium heat. Add about 2 tbsp cooking water and let bubble. Add orecchiette and cook for 1 to 2 minutes until pasta has absorbed most of liquid.

5 Gently toss cauliflower in pasta. (Be sure to include all crispy bits of garlic and red pepper flakes from the roasting pan.) Transfer to 4 serving dishes and top with equal amounts parsley and mint. Serve immediately with Parmesan.

PASTA SWAP // corn flour orecchiette (see p38) // dried brown rice shells

PROSCIUTTO, FIG & THYME RAVIOLI WITH BROWNED BUTTER

You'll never guess that these ravioli are gluten free. Remember to pre-soak your figs the night before. If you can't find lemon thyme for the filling, use regular thyme and a teaspoon of lemon zest.

INGREDIENTS

1 batch of almond & tapioca flour dough (see p40)
4oz (115g) unsalted butter
shaved Parmesan cheese, to serve

for the filling

1oz (30g) dried mission figs
2½oz (75g) soft goat cheese, room temperature
2oz (60g) cream cheese, room temperature
1 tsp finely chopped lemon thyme leaves, plus extra to garnish
1oz (30g) prosciutto slices, finely chopped
salt and freshly ground black pepper

makes **32 ravioli** // time **50 mins, plus overnight to soak** // **gluten free**

METHOD

1 To make the filling: place figs in a small, heatproof bowl. Cover with boiling water and let soak, covered, overnight. When they are plumped up, drain and squeeze to remove excess water. Chop very finely.

2 By hand, beat together goat cheese and cream cheese. Mix in figs, lemon thyme, and prosciutto. Season well with a little bit of salt and a generous amount of pepper.

3 To form ravioli, follow the instructions on page 50. Use about 1 tsp filling for each, rolling it into a small ball with your hands. You should be able to make at least 32 1-in (2.5cm) square ravioli.

4 Bring a large pot of salted water to a boil. Working a few at a time, cook ravioli in the boiling water for 2 to 3 minutes until they start to float. Use a slotted spoon to remove from water, and place on a plate lined with paper towel. Continue until all are cooked.

5 To make brown butter, in a light-colored, heavy-bottomed saucepan, melt butter over medium heat. Swirl the pan occasionally until butter bubbles. When bubbles subside, the color will start to change from yellow to golden brown. Watch it carefully as it can burn easily at this stage. When it reaches a deep golden brown color and smells nutty, immediately remove from heat and pour it into a heatproof bowl.

6 Let butter cool completely. Burnt solids will sink to the bottom of the bowl. Carefully pour off top layer of brown, clarified butter, and discard the solids at the bottom.

7 Gently reheat clarified butter in a small pan. Pour over ravioli. Top generously with Parmesan, garnish with lemon thyme, and serve immediately.

PASTA SWAP // beet & rice flour dough (see p28)

PASTA
BAKES

TURKEY & ROSEMARY BUTTERNUT SQUASH LASAGNE

This vegetable-rich lasagne uses squash rather than pasta to separate the layers. It has a complex, slightly sweet and smoky flavor that pairs well with a crisp green salad.

INGREDIENTS

4 tbsp olive oil, plus extra for greasing
1 small onion, finely chopped
1 large celery stalk, trimmed, de-ribbed, and finely chopped
1 leek, trimmed, and finely chopped
1 large garlic clove, crushed
1½lb (675g) ground dark turkey
1 tbsp rice flour
8fl oz (240ml) good quality chicken stock
2 tbsp finely chopped flat-leaf parsley
1 sprig of rosemary
salt and freshly ground black pepper
1lb (450g) thinly sliced butternut squash

for the ricotta sauce
7oz (200g) whole milk ricotta cheese
4fl oz (120ml) heavy cream
1½oz (45g) grated Parmesan cheese
1 egg
½ tbsp rice flour

serves 4–6 // time 2 hours 5 mins // gluten free

METHOD

1 To make the turkey filling: in a large, heavy-bottomed saucepan, heat 2 tbsp olive oil over medium heat. Add onion, celery, and leek. Cook for 2 to 3 minutes until soft but not brown. Add garlic and cook for 1 minute more.

2 Add remaining 2 tbsp olive oil and increase heat to high. Add turkey and cook for 3 to 4 minutes, stirring frequently, until well browned. Stir in rice flour.

3 Add chicken stock, parsley, and rosemary. Season with salt and pepper, and bring to a boil. Reduce to a simmer and cook, uncovered, for 20 minutes, occasionally stirring, until liquid reduces. Remove rosemary sprig.

4 Meanwhile, brush a griddle pan with a little olive oil. Place squash slices on griddle and cook for 1 to 2 minutes on each side until soft and with griddle marks on them.

5 Preheat the oven to 375°F (190°C). To make the ricotta sauce: in a small bowl, whisk together all ingredients. Transfer to a small saucepan and heat over medium heat, whisking constantly, until it thickens and starts to bubble. Taste and season with salt and pepper. Remove from heat.

6 To assemble the lasagne: in a 10-in (25cm) square ovenproof dish, spread one-third of turkey mixture to coat the bottom of the dish. On top of that, layer one-third of squash slices, and one-third of ricotta sauce. Repeat to make three layers total with ricotta sauce on top. Transfer to the center rack of the oven and bake, uncovered, for 45 minutes, or until golden brown. Let stand for 5 to 10 minutes before cutting and serving.

SWEET POTATO GNOCCHI & HAZELNUT GREMOLATA

The zesty flavor and crunchy texture of the hazelnut gremolata contrasts well with the soft, slightly sweet gnocchi. Creamy, rich cheese sauce makes this dish truly decadent.

INGREDIENTS

for the gnocchi dough

2 medium sweet potatoes, about 10oz (300g) in total
1 tsp very finely chopped sage leaves
1oz (30g) finely grated Parmesan cheese
salt and freshly ground black pepper
2oz (60g) sweet rice flour
2oz (60g) millet flour
2oz (60g) almond flour

for the gremolata

½oz (15g) hazelnuts, roughly chopped
1 tbsp finely chopped flat-leaf parsley
½ tsp lemon zest
1 tbsp freshly grated Parmesan cheese

for the cheese sauce

4fl oz (120ml) heavy cream
4oz (115g) grated cheese, such as Gruyère or fontina
1 tsp sweet rice flour

serves 4–6 // time 2 hrs, plus 2 hrs to cool // gluten free

METHOD

1 Preheat the oven to 450°F (230°C). To make the gnocchi dough: wash and dry sweet potatoes. Cut a small slit in skins. Place in the oven and bake for 45 minutes, or until fork-tender. Remove from the oven and let cool completely.

2 Cut cooled potatoes in half. Scoop flesh into a medium bowl and mash with a potato masher. Stir in sage and Parmesan, and season with salt and pepper. Stir in sweet rice flour, millet flour, and almond flour, mixing together well to form a soft, sticky dough. To shape the gnocchi, follow the instructions on page 58.

3 To make the gremolata: in a non-stick frying pan, dry-fry hazelnuts over medium heat for 2 minutes, stirring frequently, until golden brown in places. Remove from heat. Once cool, rub them well in a clean dish towel to remove as much of skins as possible. Set aside to cool, then finely chop.

4 Bring a large pot of salted water to a boil. In a small bowl, mix together hazelnuts, parsley, lemon zest, and Parmesan. Season well with black pepper.

5 Reduce boiling water to a simmer. Working in batches, add gnocchi to water and cook for 4 to 5 minutes until they float to the surface. Remove with a slotted spoon and place on a plate lined with paper towel to absorb water. Continue until all are cooked.

6 Pre-heat the oven to 450°F (230°C). To make the cheese sauce: add heavy cream and grated cheese to a small saucepan. Scatter sweet rice flour over the surface and whisk in. Slowly bring to a boil, stirring constantly, until sauce thickens and starts to bubble. Reduce heat to low and cook for 1 minute more until thick and smooth. Season with black pepper.

7 Grease a large, shallow, ovenproof dish. Arrange gnocchi in an even layer in the dish. Spread cheese sauce over top. Transfer to the top rack of the oven and bake, uncovered, for 10 to 12 minutes until the top is golden brown and crispy. Remove from the oven and let cool for 5 to 10 minutes. Scatter the top with hazelnut gremolata before serving.

SPINACH, BLUE CHEESE & WALNUT MANICOTTI

What seems like a lot of spinach will wilt down to very little to help make a rich, creamy filling for the manicotti. Use a mild blue cheese, as the stronger varieties can be overwhelming.

INGREDIENTS

8oz (225g) walnuts, roughly chopped
4 tbsp olive oil, plus extra for greasing
1 large white onion, finely chopped
2 garlic cloves, crushed
12oz (350g) baby spinach,
  roughly chopped
¾ cup heavy cream
6oz (175g) mild blue cheese, crumbled
salt and freshly ground black pepper
16 dried brown rice manicotti shells

for the béchamel sauce

1oz (30g) butter
1oz (30g) sweet white rice flour
1½ cups whole milk
4 tbsp grated Parmesan cheese

serves 4 // time 1 hr 55 mins // gluten free

METHOD

1 In a small, non-stick frying pan, dry-fry walnuts over medium-low heat for 2 to 3 minutes, stirring frequently, until they start to brown at the edges. Remove from heat. Once cool, rub them well in a clean dish towel to remove skins. Finely chop.

2 In a large saucepan, heat olive oil over medium heat. Add onion and cook for 3 to 4 minutes until soft, but not brown, then add garlic and cook for 1 minute more. Add spinach, increase heat to high, and stir for 1 to 2 minutes until spinach completely wilts. Add cream, allow it to boil briefly, and remove from heat. Stir in blue cheese and walnuts, season well with pepper, and set aside.

3 Cook manicotti shells in boiling, salted water according to the package instructions, and drain well. Preheat the oven to 400°F (200°C) and grease a 9 x 13-in (23 x 33cm) baking dish with olive oil. Using your fingers, stuff manicotti with spinach mixture, and place them in a single layer in the prepared dish.

4 To make the béchamel sauce: melt butter in a small, heavy-bottomed saucepan. Off the heat, whisk rice flour into butter, then gradually whisk in milk.

5 Return the pan to medium-high heat and cook, whisking constantly, for 2 to 3 minutes until mixture thickens and is starting to boil. Reduce heat to low and continue to cook for another 2 to 3 minutes, whisking occasionally. Add Parmesan and whisk until melted. Remove from heat and season well.

6 Cover manicotti with béchamel sauce and transfer to the oven. Bake for 30 minutes until the top is golden brown. Remove from the oven and let cool for at least 5 minutes before serving.

CELERIAC MACARONI & CHEESE WITH BACON

A childhood favorite gets a sophisticated update with this hearty dish. Earthy celeriac purée forms a base for the rich cream sauce, which is subtly flavored with garlic and thyme.

INGREDIENTS

1 cup whole milk

1 cup chicken stock

1 large sprig of thyme

salt and freshly ground black pepper

*1lb (450g) celeriac, peeled and cubed
(prepared weight)*

12oz (350g) dried quinoa and corn elbows

*2 tbsp olive oil, plus extra for greasing
and to toss*

1 small red onion, finely diced

4oz (115g) bacon, chopped

2 garlic cloves, crushed

3oz (85g) fontina cheese, finely grated

¼ cup whipping cream

1 tbsp finely chopped flat-leaf parsley

1oz (30g) grated Parmesan cheese

1oz (30g) white breadcrumbs

serves 4–6 // time 1 hr 40 mins

METHOD

1 Preheat the oven to 400°F (200°C). In a medium, heavy-bottomed saucepan, whisk together milk and chicken stock over medium heat. Add thyme and season well with pepper and a little salt. Add celeriac and bring to a boil, then reduce to a simmer and cook, covered, for 20 to 30 minutes until celeriac is soft. Remove from heat, discard thyme sprig, and set aside to cool.

2 While celeriac simmers, cook pasta in boiling, salted water according to the package instructions until just al dente. Drain, then rinse well under cold water. Drain again, then toss with a drizzle of olive oil to prevent sticking. Set aside to cool.

3 In a large frying pan, heat olive oil over medium heat, add onion, and cook for 2 to 3 minutes until soft, but not brown. Add bacon and cook for 5 minutes, or until brown and crispy. Reduce heat to low, stir in garlic, and cook for 1 minute more.

4 When celeriac mixture is cool, transfer to a blender or food processor, add fontina and cream, and blend until very smooth. Adjust seasoning and pour into a large mixing bowl. Add pasta, bacon mixture, and chopped parsley, and mix well to combine.

5 Grease a 9 x 13-in (23 x 33cm) baking dish with olive oil and transfer pasta to the prepared dish. In a small bowl, mix together Parmesan and breadcrumbs and season with pepper. Scatter breadcrumb mixture over the surface of pasta, and transfer to the oven. Bake for 30 minutes, or until bubbling at the edges and golden brown and crispy on top. Let cool for at least 5 minutes before serving.

PASTA SWAP // dried quinoa shells **//** dried brown rice elbows

CREAMY FONTINA & TRUFFLE LASAGNE

The sweet, creamy fontina and truffle oil make this an especially luxurious lasagne. The buttery sauce is delicious with a sharp green salad to balance the richness of the dish.

INGREDIENTS

2 tbsp olive oil

1lb (450g) cleaned, trimmed, and roughly chopped mixed mushrooms (such as cremini, portobello, oyster, and shiitake)

1 large garlic clove, crushed

12oz (340g) jar grilled artichoke halves in oil, drained and roughly chopped

2 tsp truffle oil

salt and freshly ground black pepper

1 batch of spinach & millet flour dough (see p30), formed into lasagne (see p48)

for the sauce

2oz (60g) unsalted butter

2oz (60g) sweet white rice flour

18fl oz (550ml) whole milk

5oz (140g) fontina cheese, roughly grated

serves 6 // time 1 hr 20 mins // gluten free // vegetarian

METHOD

1 Preheat the oven to 400°F (200°C). To make the filling: in a large frying pan, heat olive oil over high heat. Working in two batches, partially cook mushrooms for 3 to 4 minutes, turning often. Recombine the batches and add garlic. Cook for 1 minute more.

2 Add artichokes and truffle oil. Season well with salt and pepper. Stir, then set aside to cool.

3 To make the sauce: in a heavy-bottomed saucepan, melt butter over medium heat. Remove from heat and whisk in rice flour. Gradually whisk in milk. Return the pan to heat and cook, whisking constantly, for 2 to 3 minutes until mixture thickens and starts to boil. Reduce heat to low and continue to cook for 2 to 3 minutes, whisking occasionally. Finally, add two-thirds of fontina, and whisk until melted. Remove from heat and season well with salt and pepper.

4 To assemble the lasagne: in 9 x 13-in (23 x 33cm) baking dish, spread one-fourth of sauce to coat the bottom of the dish. On top of that, layer one-third of filling, and a single layer of lasagne sheets. Then layer with another one-fourth of sauce, one-third of filling, and a single layer of lasagne sheets. Top with another one-fourth of sauce, remaining mushroom mixture, and a final layer of lasagne sheets.

5 Cover the top with remaining sauce and remaining one-third of fontina. Transfer to the middle rack of the oven and bake for 40 to 45 minutes until well browned and cooked through. Let stand 10 to 15 minutes before cutting and serving.

PASTA SWAP // chickpea flour lasagne (see p34) // dried brown rice lasagne

CITRUS ZUCCHINI CANNELLONI WITH GOAT CHEESE

Griddling the zucchini slices helps them to become soft and easy to roll. The lightly charred flavor is a nice addition to the cheesy and lemony filling. Serve with a crisp green salad.

INGREDIENTS

olive oil, for greasing and to serve

2 fat zucchini, about 10oz (300g) each, trimmed and cut into 12 thin slices lengthwise with a mandoline

2oz (60g) pine nuts

7oz (200g) soft goat cheese, room temperature

2 tbsp finely chopped basil, plus whole leaves to garnish

zest of 1 small or ½ large lemon

salt and freshly ground black pepper

for the cheese sauce

½oz (15g) unsalted butter

½oz (15g) sweet rice flour

3½fl oz (100ml) whole milk

1oz (30g) strong cheese, such as Cheddar, grated

serves 4 // time 55 mins // gluten free // vegetarian

METHOD

1 Heat a cast-iron griddle and lightly brush with olive oil. Griddle zucchini slices for 1 to 2 minutes on each side until soft and lightly marked with grill marks. At the same time, in a non-stick frying pan, dry-fry pine nuts over medium heat for 2 to 3 minutes, turning frequently, until golden brown. Set aside to cool. Blot any excess moisture with a paper towel once cool.

2 In a small bowl, beat together goat cheese, basil, lemon zest, and pine nuts. Season well with salt and pepper.

3 To assemble the cannelloni: portion a large, walnut-sized spoonful of goat cheese mixture and place on the zucchini slice. Spread out the cheese along the length of the slice. Roll slice up. Place in a lightly oiled shallow ovenproof dish. Repeat to assemble remaining cannelloni.

4 Preheat the oven to 450°F (230°C). To make the cheese sauce: in a small saucepan, melt butter over medium heat. Remove from heat and whisk in rice flour. Continue to whisk, slowly adding in milk. Return to heat and slowly bring to a boil, whisking frequently, until mixture thickens. Reduce heat to low and continue to cook for 2 to 3 minutes. Season well with salt and pepper and add most of grated cheese, reserving some to sprinkle over top. Whisk sauce until cheese melts, adding more milk if needed to help achieve pourable consistency. Remove from heat.

5 Pour sauce over cannelloni and top with remaining grated cheese. Transfer to the top rack of the oven. Cook, uncovered, for 15 to 20 minutes until the top is golden brown and cannelloni are cooked through. Remove from the oven and let cool for 10 minutes, or until cheese settles. Garnish with basil and a drizzle of olive oil, and serve.

SMOKED TURKEY & SHIITAKE TETRAZZINI

Smoked turkey can be bought ready-made in most delis. Look for the large wings, which have dark meat that lends a deeper flavor to the finished dish.

INGREDIENTS

8oz (225g) dried chickpea spaghetti

salt and freshly ground black pepper

2 tbsp olive oil, plus extra for greasing and to toss

1 white onion, finely sliced

4oz (115g) shiitake mushrooms, cleaned, trimmed, and finely sliced

2 garlic cloves, crushed

2 tbsp butter

2 tbsp tapioca flour

½ cup white wine

1½ cups chicken stock

¼ cup heavy cream

2 tbsp sour cream

2oz (60g) grated Parmesan cheese

1 tbsp finely chopped flat-leaf parsley

7oz (200g) finely shredded meat from cooked, smoked turkey wings

for the topping

1 tbsp finely chopped flat-leaf parsley

1oz (30g) fresh gluten-free breadcrumbs

1oz (30g) grated Parmesan cheese

serves 4–6 // time 1 hr 35 mins // gluten free

METHOD

1 Preheat the oven to 400°F (200°C) and grease a 9 x 13-in (23 x 33cm) baking dish with olive oil. Break dried spaghetti into a more manageable length to eat. Cook pasta according to the package instructions in boiling, salted water, but remove from water just before fully cooked. Drain, rinse under cold water, and drain again. Toss with a drizzle of olive oil to prevent sticking.

2 In a large, non-stick frying pan, heat 1 tbsp olive oil over medium heat. Add onion and cook for 2 to 3 minutes. Add shiitake mushrooms and remaining 1 tbsp olive oil, toss well to combine, and cook for another 5 minutes until mushrooms soften and begin to brown. Add garlic and cook for 1 minute more. Add butter and allow it to melt.

3 Remove the pan from heat and sprinkle in tapioca flour. Stir it in well, then stir in wine. Return to heat and add chicken stock. Heat mixture until boiling and thickened. Add cream and cook for 1 minute more. Remove from heat and stir in sour cream, Parmesan, and parsley. Season well and fold in shredded turkey.

4 Add spaghetti to turkey and sauce, and toss to combine. Transfer it to the prepared baking dish.

5 To make the topping: in a small bowl, mix together all ingredients. Sprinkle over the surface of pasta. Transfer to the oven and bake for 30 minutes until the surface is golden brown. Let cool for 5 to 10 minutes before serving.

PASTA SWAP // chickpea flour spaghetti (see p34) // dried spelt spaghetti

BAKED ROTINI WITH SAUSAGE, KALE & MASCARPONE

The earthy, rustic quality of chickpea pasta pairs well with the hearty flavor of tomato sauce made with sausage and kale. Creamy mascarpone brings the dish together and balances the heat of the red pepper flakes.

INGREDIENTS

2 tbsp olive oil, plus extra for greasing and to toss

1 small yellow onion, finely diced

10oz (300g) ground Italian sausage meat (or Italian sausage links, meat removed from casing and crumbled)

2 garlic cloves, crushed

¼ tsp red pepper flakes

14oz (400g) crushed tomatoes

freshly ground black pepper

2oz (60g) de-ribbed and finely chopped kale

10oz (300g) dried chickpea rotini

4oz (115g) mascarpone

serves 4–6 // time 1 hr 20 mins // gluten free

METHOD

1 Preheat the oven to 400°F (200°C) and grease a 9 x 13-in (23 x 33cm) baking dish with olive oil. In a medium, heavy-bottomed saucepan, heat olive oil over medium heat. Add onion and cook for 2 to 3 minutes until soft, but not brown. Add sausage meat and cook for 3 to 4 minutes until browned. Reduce heat to low, stir in garlic and red pepper flakes, and cook for 1 minute more.

2 Add crushed tomatoes to the pan and season well with pepper. Bring to a boil, then reduce to a simmer and cook, uncovered, for 20 minutes until sauce reduces and thickens. Remove the pan from heat and stir in kale. Cover and allow kale to wilt.

3 Meanwhile, cook pasta according to the package instructions, removing it from heat just before fully cooked. Drain, then rinse under cold water. Drain again, toss with a drizzle of olive oil to prevent sticking, and set aside in a large bowl to cool.

4 Pour sauce over cooled pasta and mix together well. Add mascarpone and stir again to combine. Pour pasta mixture into the prepared baking dish, transfer to the oven, and bake for 30 minutes until the surface is golden brown in places. Let cool for at least 5 minutes before serving.

PASTA SWAP // dried red lentil penne // dried quinoa rotini

PANCETTA & BROCCOLI EINKORN PASTA BAKE

This cheesy and savory pasta bake is filling and delicious. Use either broccoli rabe or baby broccoli here. If you can find neither, slice regular broccoli into long, thin stems.

INGREDIENTS

salt and freshly ground black pepper

4oz (115g) trimmed broccoli rabe, cut into 3-in (7.5cm) pieces

9oz (250g) dried einkorn pasta, such as rotini or other small shape

2 tbsp olive oil, plus extra for greasing

1 small red onion, finely chopped

4oz (115g) diced pancetta

1 large garlic clove, crushed

4oz (115g) cream cheese

4oz (115g) soft goat cheese

2 tbsp sweet rice flour

1 heaped tbsp finely chopped flat-leaf parsley

serves 4 // time **50 mins**

METHOD

1 Preheat the oven to 400°F (200°C). Prepare a bowl of iced water. Boil a large pot of salted water and cook broccoli rabe for 1 minute. Remove with a slotted spoon and submerge in iced water to refresh. Drain and set aside.

2 Cook pasta in the same boiling water according to the package instructions until just al dente. Drain and rinse under cold water, reserving 1½ cups cooking water. Set pasta aside to let drain and cool completely.

3 In a large saucepan, heat olive oil over medium heat. Add red onion and cook for 3 to 5 minutes, stirring occasionally, until soft but not brown. Add pancetta and cook for 2 to 3 minutes until starting to crisp. Stir in garlic and cook for 1 minute more.

4 Add cream cheese and goat cheese to the pan, reduce heat to low, and stir constantly until cheese melts. Add 1 cup reserved cooking water, and stir well. Scatter sweet rice flour over surface and whisk in. Raise heat to medium and continue to cook, stirring frequently, until sauce thickens. Add reserved cooking water as needed to make sauce fluid enough to pour. Season with salt and pepper to taste.

5 Stir in pasta, broccoli, and parsley. Transfer mixture to a deep 8 x 10-in (20 x 25cm) ovenproof dish, lightly greased with olive oil. Transfer to the top rack of the oven and bake, uncovered, for 15 to 20 minutes until the top is golden brown in places. Let stand for 5 minutes before serving.

PASTA SWAP // dried brown rice rotini // dried quinoa penne // buckwheat flour farfalle (see p36)

SUMAC ROASTED SALMON, FENNEL & RYE PASTA

Taking inspiration from a classic smoked salmon on rye sandwich, the earthy taste of rye pasta provides a perfect foil to the gentle flavor of salmon, sharp sour cream, and lemony sumac.

INGREDIENTS

7oz (200g) fennel
1 tbsp olive oil, plus extra for greasing
salt and freshly ground black pepper
12oz (350g) salmon fillet
9oz (250g) dried rye trumpets or rotini

for the sauce

1 tbsp unsalted butter
1 tbsp all-purpose flour
8fl oz (240ml) seafood stock
2oz (60g) cream cheese
2oz (60g) sour cream
1 tbsp finely chopped dill, plus extra to garnish
1 tsp sumac

serves 4–6 // time 1 hr

METHOD

1 Preheat the oven to 400°F (200°C). Line a baking sheet with parchment paper. Trim fennel, reserving fronds for garnish, and slice bulb in half. Cut each half into thin slices and toss fennel in olive oil. Spread out on half of the sheet. Season well with salt and pepper.

2 Season salmon and place on the other half of the sheet. Transfer the sheet to the top rack of the oven and roast for 10 to 12 minutes until salmon is cooked and fennel has softened. Remove from the oven and let cool slightly. Then use a fork to flake salmon into chunks. Set aside salmon and fennel and discard salmon skin. Turn the oven up to 425°F (220°C).

3 Meanwhile, cook pasta according to the package instructions until just al dente. Drain and rinse under cold water, and set aside to cool.

4 To make the sauce: melt butter in a medium, heavy-bottomed saucepan. Remove from heat and whisk in flour. Gradually whisk in seafood stock, then return to heat. Bring to a boil, whisking continuously, until sauce thickens and bubbles. Whisk in cream cheese, then remove from heat. Whisk in sour cream, dill, and ½ tsp sumac. Season very well with salt and pepper.

5 In the saucepan, toss together pasta, salmon, fennel, and sauce. Transfer mixture to a large, shallow, greased, ovenproof dish and scatter the top with remaining ½ tsp sumac. Transfer to the middle rack of the oven and bake for 15 to 20 minutes until golden brown in places. Let cool for 5 minutes, garnish with chopped fennel fronds and dill, and serve.

PASTA SWAP // dried whole wheat rotini // dried einkorn penne // spelt & chestnut flour orecchiette (see p42)

SPAETZLE & PANCETTA AU GRATIN

This cozy, creamy dish is comfort food at its best. Homemade spaetzle are tossed with a savory cheese sauce and broiled until browned and bubbling. Enjoy this rich dish with a crisp green salad.

INGREDIENTS

2 tbsp olive oil, plus extra for greasing
1 small red onion, finely chopped
4oz (115g) diced pancetta
¼ cup heavy cream
4oz (115g) grated Gruyère cheese
salt and freshly ground black pepper

for the spaetzle batter

6oz (175g) spelt flour
6oz (175g) all-purpose white flour
1 tsp salt
1 tsp baking powder
3 eggs
¾–1 cup whole milk

serves 4 // time 55 mins

METHOD

1 To make the spaetzle batter: in a large bowl, whisk together spelt flour, all-purpose flour, salt, and baking powder. Beat in eggs and ¾ cup milk to form a very thick batter. If necessary, add remaining ¼ cup milk, a tablespoon at a time, and stir vigorously until bubbles form. Cook spaetzle according to the instructions on page 60 and let cool.

2 In a large, non-stick frying pan, heat olive oil over medium heat. Add red onion and cook for 5 to 8 minutes until soft but not brown. Add pancetta and cook for 5 to 7 minutes, stirring occasionally, until pancetta is crisp. Remove from heat.

3 Preheat the broiler to high. Grease a 9 x 13-in (23 x 33cm) baking dish. Add pancetta and onions to spaetzle, along with cream and most of Gruyère. Season well. Gently mix to combine and spread in the baking dish. Top with remaining Gruyère, transfer to the oven, and broil on high until hot, bubbling, and crisp on top. Serve immediately.

PASTA SICILIANA WITH BURRATA & ANCHOVIES

A simple tomato sauce is given an aromatic flavor boost with the addition of salty anchovies and piquant olives and capers. Rich and buttery burrata balances the flavor profile.

INGREDIENTS

2 tbsp olive oil, plus extra for greasing and to toss

1 white onion, finely chopped

2 garlic cloves, crushed

2oz (55g) tin anchovies, chopped, plus oil from tin

28oz (794g) can crushed tomatoes

salt and freshly ground black pepper

10oz (300g) dried chickpea rotini

16 black olives, pitted and roughly chopped

1½ tbsp capers, rinsed and dried

2 tbsp roughly chopped basil leaves

4oz (115g) burrata, roughly torn

serves 4 // time 1 hr 20 mins // gluten free

METHOD

1 In a medium, heavy-bottomed saucepan, heat olive oil over medium heat. Add onion and cook for 5 minutes, or until soft, but not brown. Add garlic and cook for 1 minute more, then add anchovies and oil and stir until they start to break up.

2 Add crushed tomatoes and some pepper to the pan and bring to a boil. Reduce to a simmer and cook, uncovered, for 30 minutes, or until sauce reduces and thickens.

3 Meanwhile, cook pasta according to the package instructions until just al dente. Drain, rinse under cold water, and drain again. Toss with a drizzle of olive oil to prevent sticking. Set aside in a large bowl and let cool.

4 Preheat the oven to 400°F (200°C) and grease a 9 x 13-in (23 x 33cm) baking dish with olive oil. Remove tomato sauce from heat and stir in olives, capers, basil, and burrata. Season well with plenty of pepper and a little salt. Mix in cooled pasta and spread out in the prepared dish, making sure that burrata is evenly distributed. Transfer to the oven and bake for 25 to 30 minutes until crisp and golden brown on top. Let rest for 5 minutes before serving.

PASTA SWAP // dried red lentil fusilli // dried green lentil penne

LAMB & FETA PASTITSIO

This classic Greek dish is best served at room temperature as the pasta really holds its shape once cooled. Cut into neat, layered wedges and serve with a crisp green salad.

INGREDIENTS

salt and freshly ground black pepper
1lb (450g) dried brown rice penne
4oz (115g) feta cheese, finely crumbled
2 egg whites, beaten until frothy (reserve yolks for béchamel sauce)

for the lamb sauce

2 tbsp olive oil, plus extra for greasing
1 small onion, finely diced
1 celery stalk, trimmed, de-ribbed, and finely diced
1 carrot, peeled and finely diced
1lb (450g) ground lamb
2 garlic cloves, crushed

4fl oz (120ml) red wine
4fl oz (120ml) good quality beef stock
14oz (400g) crushed tomatoes
½ tsp dried mint
⅛ tsp cinnamon

for the béchamel sauce

1oz (30g) unsalted butter, plus extra for greasing
1oz (30g) sweet rice flour
16fl oz (500ml) full-fat milk
pinch of ground nutmeg

serves 6 // time 1 hr 30 mins // gluten free

METHOD

1 Bring a medium, heavy-bottomed pot of salted water to a boil. Cook pasta for 3 to 4 minutes less than specified by the package instructions so it is still very al dente. Drain and rinse under cold water. Transfer pasta to a medium bowl. Let cool.

2 To make the lamb sauce: in the same pot, heat olive oil over medium heat. Add onion, celery, and carrot, and cook for 3 to 4 minutes until soft but not brown. Add lamb, raise heat to high, and cook until browned, stirring frequently. Add garlic and cook for 1 minute more.

3 Add wine, beef stock, crushed tomatoes, mint, and cinnamon. Season generously with salt and pepper. Bring to a boil, then reduce to a simmer. Cook, uncovered, for 30 minutes, or until sauce reduces and thickens.

4 When pasta is cool, stir in feta and egg whites. Season with salt and pepper.

5 To make the béchamel sauce: in a small, heavy-bottomed saucepan, melt butter over medium heat. Remove from heat and whisk in flour. Then gradually whisk in milk.

6 Return to heat and cook, whisking constantly, for 2 to 3 minutes until mixture thickens and starts to boil. Reduce heat to low and continue to cook for 2 to 3 minutes, whisking occasionally. Season with salt, pepper, and nutmeg. Remove from heat and whisk in egg yolks.

7 Preheat the oven to 400°F (200°C). Grease a deep 9 x 13-in (23 x 33cm) dish with butter. To assemble: spread half of penne mixture in the dish, and pack down well. Cover with lamb sauce, spreading it out evenly. Top with remaining penne mixture, and pack down to create an even layer. Finally, top with béchamel sauce.

8 Transfer dish to the center rack of the oven and bake, uncovered, for 35 to 45 minutes until cooked through and well browned on top. Remove from the oven and let cool for 30 minutes before serving.

PASTA SWAP // dried quinoa penne // dried einkorn penne

SWEET POTATO & ROSEMARY NOODLE KUGEL

This twist on the traditional Jewish baked casserole is made with spiralized sweet potato instead of egg noodles. It can be served warm or at room temperature and reheats well.

INGREDIENTS

2 tbsp olive oil

1 tbsp butter

1 large white onion, very finely sliced

3 eggs

1 tbsp finely chopped rosemary

salt and freshly ground black pepper

2lb (900g) sweet potatoes, peeled and spiralized

2 tbsp tapioca flour

serves 4–6 // time 1 hr 25 mins // gluten free // vegetarian

METHOD

1 Preheat the oven to 350°F (180°C). In an ovenproof skillet, heat olive oil and butter over medium-low heat. Add onion and cook for 5 minutes, or until soft but not brown. Remove the pan from heat and set aside.

2 In a large bowl, beat eggs until whites and yolks are well combined. Add rosemary and season well. Add spiralized sweet potatoes and onions to the bowl and toss to combine. Sprinkle tapioca flour over mixture and toss once more.

3 Tip mixture into the skillet and pack it down well. Bake on the top rack of the oven for 1 hour, or until sweet potato is golden brown on top and soft when pierced with a knife.

4 Remove from the oven and let sit for at least 5 minutes before turning it out onto a plate and cutting into wedges to serve.

NOODLE SWAP // spiralized butternut squash

GREEN LENTIL LASAGNE WITH ROASTED VEGETABLES

Although the entire dish takes a couple of hours to prepare, most of the time is hands off. To cut down the preparation time, the vegetables can be roasted up to 2 days ahead and chilled until needed.

INGREDIENTS

1 eggplant, diced, about 1lb (450g) in total

1 red pepper, diced

1 yellow pepper, diced

4 tbsp olive oil

salt and freshly ground black pepper

1 small zucchini, diced

1 small red onion, diced

1lb (450g) cherry tomatoes, halved

2 garlic cloves, crushed

8oz (225g) dried green lentil lasagne, no-boil variety

for the béchamel sauce

3 tbsp butter

1½oz (45g) sweet white rice flour

2 cups whole milk

3 tbsp grated Parmesan cheese

serves 4 // time 2 hrs 20 mins // gluten free

METHOD

1 Preheat the oven to 425°F (220°C). On a rimmed baking sheet, toss eggplant and peppers with olive oil, season well, and spread out in a single layer. Transfer to the oven and roast for 20 minutes.

2 Add zucchini, red onion, cherry tomatoes, and garlic to the baking sheet, along with peppers, and toss together. Roast again for 25 to 30 minutes until vegetables are soft and browning at the edges. Remove from the oven and set aside to cool. Turn down the oven to 400°F (200°C).

3 To make the béchamel sauce: melt butter in a small, heavy-bottomed saucepan. Remove from heat and whisk in rice flour, then gradually whisk in milk. Return the pan to heat and cook, whisking constantly, for 2 to 3 minutes until mixture thickens and is starting to boil. Reduce heat to low and continue to cook for 2 to 3 minutes, whisking occasionally. Add Parmesan and whisk until melted. Remove from heat and season well.

4 To assemble: spread a quarter of sauce at the bottom of a 9 x 13-in (23 x 33cm) baking dish. Spread a third of vegetable mixture on top of sauce in a single layer, and top with a layer of lasagne sheets. Top with another quarter of sauce, another third of vegetables, and another layer of lasagne sheets. Finish with half of remaining sauce, all remaining vegetables, and a final layer of lasagne sheets. Cover the top with remaining sauce.

5 Cover lasagne, transfer to the oven, and bake for 30 minutes. Then uncover and bake for another 10 to 15 minutes until well browned on top and cooked through. Remove from the oven and let rest for 5 to 10 minutes before serving.

PASTA SWAP // spinach & millet flour lasagne (see p30) // dried brown rice lasagne

SUBSTITUTING PASTA TYPES

If you can't find the pasta called for in a recipe, or don't want to make your own dough, you can easily swap one form of pasta for another.

SWAPPING ONE FRESH PASTA DOUGH FOR ANOTHER

All of the dough recipes in this book have roughly the same yield, so a batch of one dough can be swapped for another. However, it is important to consider taste and texture when swapping pasta doughs. A more rustic dough with a pronounced flavor, such as buckwheat, may not work well in a recipe that calls for a lighter, milder dough, such as almond and tapioca flour.

SWAPPING DRIED PASTA FOR FRESH PASTA

Yields for homemade doughs can vary, but a good rule of thumb is to substitute 10 to 12 ounces (300–350g) of dried, packaged pasta for 1 batch of homemade dough. You can also use this conversion if you want to use homemade pasta in place of a packaged pasta.

SWAPPING VEGETABLE NOODLES FOR PASTA

Replacing pasta with vegetable noodles works best when the recipe calls for tossing a sauce with pasta or noodles, and is a great way to reduce the carbs in a dish and add nutritional value. However, it is not recommended to use vegetable noodles in place of pasta in baked dishes and soups because the noodles can become mushy and overcooked.

SWAPPING ONE DRIED PASTA FOR ANOTHER

There are many types of alternative pastas, some of which are more readily available than others. If you are unable to find a particular dried pasta, you can substitute an equivalent amount of another variety. For the best results, choose a substitute that is similar in shape, flavor, and texture to the pasta called for in the recipe.

CHOOSING YOUR STORE-BOUGHT SUBSTITUTE

With an influx of pasta alternatives on the market, pre-packaged options are an easy way to prepare a healthful meal. If you're unable to find the exact type of pasta called for in a recipe, or if you would like to try a different variety, refer to the following table for substitutions of comparable taste and texture. Remember that using a similar shape will yield the best results.

Pasta or noodle variety	Good substitutes
Black bean pasta	Red lentil pasta
Brown rice pasta	Quinoa pasta
Buckwheat noodles	Spelt pasta, einkorn pasta
Chickpea pasta	Brown rice pasta
Corn pasta	Quinoa pasta, millet pasta
Edamame pasta	Green lentil pasta
Einkorn pasta	Brown rice pasta, buckwheat noodles
Glass noodles (also called cellophane, bean thread, or mung bean noodles)	Rice vermicelli, kelp noodles
Green lentil pasta	Red lentil pasta
Kelp noodles	Glass noodles, shirataki noodles
Millet pasta	Chickpea pasta, quinoa pasta, brown rice pasta
Quinoa pasta	Corn pasta
Rice vermicelli or rice noodles	Shirataki noodles, sweet potato vermicelli
Rye pasta	Einkorn pasta, spelt pasta
Shirataki noodles	Kelp noodles, rice vermicelli
Sweet potato vermicelli	Rice vermicelli

INDEX

Editor: Alexandra Elliott
Senior editors: Ann Barton and Kathryn Meeker
Book designer: Hannah Moore
Senior art editor: Glenda Fisher
Photographer: Charlotte Tolhurst
Jacket designer: Steven Marsden
Managing editor: Stephanie Farrow
Managing art editor: Christine Keilty
Publisher: Mike Sanders

First American Edition, 2018
Published in the United States by DK Publishing
6081 E. 82nd Street, Indianapolis, Indiana 46250

Copyright © 2018 Dorling Kindersley Limited
A Penguin Random House Company
18 19 20 21   10 9 8 7 6 5 4 3 2 1
01–308488–Feb/2018

Published in the United States by Dorling Kindersley Limited.

ISBN: 978-1-4654-6994-6

Library of Congress Catalog Number: 2017948326

Note: This publication contains the opinions and ideas of its
author(s). It is intended to provide helpful and informative
material on the subject matter covered. It is sold with the
understanding that the author(s) and publisher are not
engaged in rendering professional services in the book. If the
reader requires personal assistance or advice, a competent
professional should be consulted. The author(s) and publisher
specifically disclaim any responsibility for any liability, loss, or risk,
personal or otherwise, which is incurred as a consequence,
directly or indirectly, of the use and application of any of the
contents of this book.

Trademarks: All terms mentioned in this book that are known to
be or are suspected of being trademarks or service marks have
been appropriately capitalized. Alpha Books, DK, and Penguin
Random House LLC cannot attest to the accuracy of this
information. Use of a term in this book should not be regarded
as affecting the validity of any trademark or service mark.

DK books are available at special discounts when purchased in
bulk for sales promotions, premiums, fund-raising, or educational
use. For details, contact: DK Publishing Special Markets,
345 Hudson Street, New York, New York 10014 or
SpecialSales@dk.com.

Printed and bound in China

All images © Dorling Kindersley Limited
For further information see: www.dkimages.com

A WORLD OF IDEAS:
SEE ALL THERE IS TO KNOW
www.dk.com

336140805*61615*

ABOUT THE AUTHOR

British-born Caroline Bretherton has spent more
than 20 years following her passion for food in many
capacities within the food industry. After running a
highly successful catering company and café in the
heart of London's Notting Hill, her career soon grew
to include the UK television market, both as a guest
chef and co-presenter of various programs within
the Food Network family.

Following a break to concentrate on her young family,
Caroline returned to the food business as the "Family
Food Writer" for *The Times Weekend Magazine*. Her
writing took off, and she soon produced her first book,
The Kitchen Garden Cookbook, published in 2011.

She has since authored *Step-by-Step Baking* (2011),
The Pie Book (2013), *Family Kitchen Cookbook* (2013),
The American Cookbook (2014), *Desserts* (2015), *Super
Clean Super Foods* (2017), and *Sprouted!* (2017). All her
books have been published internationally by DK and
translated into several languages. Caroline has also
contributed recipes to *The Daily Telegraph* and worked
with well-known nutritionist Jane Clarke to contribute
recipes to her book *Complete Family Nutrition* (2014).

Caroline lives in North Carolina with her husband
and two sons, where she continues to write,
teach, and above all, cook.

AUTHOR'S THANKS

I would like to thank all at DK, both in the UK and
US, who helped shape a book which has been
simultaneously one of the most challenging and
satisfying I have ever had the pleasure of writing.
Thanks especially go to Ann Barton and Alexandra
Elliott for their tireless work and encouragement. To
my husband Luke, who happily ate bowl after bowl
of pasta with no discernible lack of enthusiasm, and
to my two sons Gabriel and Isaac, who, for the most
part, ate beyond their comfort zones and discovered
some wonderful new dishes along the way.

PUBLISHER'S THANKS

Food stylist: Maud Eden
Recipe tester: Trish Sebben Malone
Proofreader: Laura Caddell
Indexer: Heather McNeill